The Political Economy of Low Carbon Transformation

Deep reductions in energy use and carbon emissions will not be possible within political economies that are driven by the capitalist imperatives of growth, commodification and individualization. As such, it has now become necessary to understand the relationship between capitalism and the emergence of high-energy habits.

Using the examples of home energy, transport and food, *The Political Economy of Low Carbon Transformation* articulates the relationship between the politics of economic expansion and the formation of high-energy habits at the level of family and household. The book elaborates a theory of habit and how it can contribute to this relationship. It critiques mainstream green economy and green energy prescriptions for low carbon transformation that take economic growth for granted and ignore habits formed in a material world designed and built for high energy use. The book explores the growing number of communities around the world that are engaged in collaborative efforts to reform their community and household habits in ways that are less environmentally intrusive. It assesses their potential to make an impact on national and urban low carbon political agendas.

The book is aimed at a large and growing interdisciplinary audience interested in the relationship between political economy, consumption and sustainability.

Harold Wilhite is Professor of Social Anthropology at the Centre for Development and the Environment, University of Oslo, Norway.

Routledge Studies in Low Carbon Development

The Political Economy of Low Carbon Transformation

Breaking the habits of capitalism

Harold Wilhite

LONDON AND NEW YORK

First published 2016
by Routledge

2 Park Square, Milton Park, Abingdon, Oxfordshire OX14 4RN
711 Third Avenue, New York, NY 10017

Routledge is an imprint of the Taylor & Francis Group, an informa business

First issued in paperback 2017

British Library Cataloguing in Publication Data
A catalogue record for this book is available from the British Library

Library of Congress Cataloging in Publication Data
Names: Wilhite, Harold, 1946- author.
Title: The political economy of low carbon transformation : breaking the habits of capitalism / Harold Wilhite.
Description: New York : Routledge, 2016. | Includes bibliographical references.
Identifiers: LCCN 2015042422| ISBN 9781138817173 (hb) | ISBN 9781315745787 (ebook)
Subjects: LCSH: Consumption (Economics) | Energy consumption--Climatic factors. | Clean energy. | Carbon dioxide mitigation.
Classification: LCC HB801 .W474 2016 | DDC 333.79/13--dc23
LC record available at http://lccn.loc.gov/2015042422

ISBN: 978-1-138-81717-3 (hbk)
ISBN: 978-0-8153-5562-5 (pbk)

Typeset in Sabon
by Taylor & Francis Books

Contents

Figures

Acknowledgement

I want to sincerely thank Michael Seltzer for his support throughout the research and writing of the book and for his valuable comments on the text. I want to also thank Dale Southerton and Monica Guillen-Royo for reading, commenting and making excellent suggestions to parts of the text. Thanks also to my colleagues at the University of Oslo's Centre for Development and Environment (SUM) for their collaboration and support on projects related to the theme of this book, with special thanks to SUM's Director Kristi Anne Stølen for generously providing time and resources for research and writing. I want to also thank my brilliant wife, Dr Zehlia Babaci Wilhite, for her support and my three wonderful children, Paul, Alexandre and Kahena.

1 Introduction

From the mid-twentieth century global energy use and climate emissions have grown in step with growing national economies. While methane, hydro-fluorocarbons and other pollutants contribute to climate perturbation, the single major contribution to climate change is related to the emissions of carbon dioxide (CO_2) from the conversion of fossil fuels to useful energy. With virtually every day that passes, new research results are published on climate-related problems and risks. The most recent projections from a number of different sources are converging on a likely global temperature rise of four degrees Celsius or more within the next 25 years and that this will have major impacts on micro-climates; on Arctic and Antarctic ice with consequent effects on sea levels and ocean chemistry (Trusel et al. 2015); severe disturbance of forest ecosystems and species death, with half of global species dying out by 2050 (Lynas 2007); as well as potential devastating effects on food production and food harvesting, both on land and in oceans. It is not my intention to review and assess all of these potentially devastating consequences for both humans and non-humans, but the most recent research on polar ice is, literally, chilling. In an article recently published in Nature, Trusel et al. (2015) found that should the global temperature increase to around 3°C above the pre-industrial era, the ice shelves that hold back the continental ice sheets would dissolve over the next few centuries. Should climate gas emissions not be significantly reduced over the next century, this would trigger a collapse that would go on for thousands of years, raising sea levels by as much as three meters by the year 2300. The authors predict that our descendants living in the year 5000 will continue to suffer the consequences of today's fossil fuel burning, as sea levels continue to rise up to nine meters above current levels. These findings graphically illustrate the accuracy of the conclusions of the most recent IPCC (2014) report: 'failure to rapidly reduce climate-gas emissions will result in severe, pervasive and irreversible impacts for people and ecosystems'.

The report of the World Commission on the Environment (WCED 1987) put climate change on the international political agenda four decades ago. The report was to have a significant impact on global, national and local efforts to reduce energy and climate emissions. The report indicated that in order to prevent severe climate change global carbon emissions would need to be reduced by

80 percent within a half century (the report assigned 60 percent reductions to the rich countries of the world and 20 percent to developing countries). Against this background, it is noteworthy that in the period from 1990 to 2010, global carbon emissions grew by 60 percent. In the USA there has been a slight decline in total emissions from an extremely high starting point compared to the rest of the world. US CO_2 per capita emissions continue to be the highest in the world (three times the per capita French emission level, and ten times that of India). This slight decline does not account for the outsourcing of emissions to other parts of the world through global imports. Sixty percent of all goods consumed in the USA are now produced elsewhere (CSE 2015). In Europe, with mixed economies and strong ambitions to increase energy efficiency, energy use has declined by 20 percent since 1990 and overall climate emissions declined by 23 percent. However, much of this decline is due to deep reductions in energy use in the former Eastern European countries after the fall of the Soviet Union in 1989, as well as minimal economic growth after 2005 due to the economic recession. Europe has also exported emission generation to other parts of the world. Seventy percent of European consumer goods are now produced outside Europe, mainly in Asia. The European Environmental Agency (EEA 2015) predicts that energy use and carbon emissions will only decline slightly in the next 25 years. Measured against what was known to be needed in 1992, the low carbon transformation can thus far be declared a failure. While the rich countries of the world have barely been able to stabilize C02 emissions, the emissions from the 'emerging' countries, including China, India and Brazil, have grown rapidly.

My argument in this book is that deep reductions in energy use and carbon emissions will not be possible within political economies saturated by the capitalist imperatives of growth, commodification and individualization. I will argue in the coming chapters that the fine-tuning of capitalism will not be sufficient to bring society and ecology into balance. A healthy ecosystem will only come about through a reduction in economic growth and through a softening of the other imperatives of capitalism, including private ownership, market-driven consumption and the overt objective to encourage product turnover. This will mean a significant change of focus from mainstream low carbon strategies that take for granted that capitalism is the formula for progress and prosperity and aim to fine-tune and reshape capitalism in ways that will make it more environmentally benign. Where the argument in this book will depart from recent critiques of within-capitalism low carbon strategies is to draw attention to the high energy and high carbon habits that have formed in capitalist societies. I will make the case that capitalism as a societally organizing system has over several generations in the now rich countries of the world fostered materially dense and carbon-intensive habits that are deeply rooted in societal norms, commercial discourses, materialities and experiential knowledge. For a number of generations, many of us in the rich countries of the world have tacitly accepted the logic of capitalism and its association of the good life with the ownership of more and bigger homes, cars, household appliances and other commodities, the routine use of which is spurred on by an ever increasing tempo of work and consumption. I will argue that the achievement of a low-energy and climate-friendly political economy will demand breaking and reforming these collectively reinforced and individually enacted habits.

There are a growing number of academic critiques of capitalist political economy from an ecological perspective (for example Prugh et al. 2000; Hamilton 2003; Jackson 2009; Patel 2009). Blundorn and Welsh (2007: 186) capture the essence of this critique when they write 'that the capitalist principles of infinite economic growth and wealth accumulation are ecologically, socially, politically and culturally unsustainable and destructive'. In the recent 'State of the World' report by the World Watch Institute, entitled *Is Sustainability Still Possible?* (WWI 2013), an impressive set of contributors state decisively that a significant reduction in the environmental impacts of economic activity will not be possible within the current economic growth paradigm. I intend to review and support these arguments, but will make the case that in order to make a low carbon transformation a focus on changes at the top – in the growth politics of capitalism – *must* be supplemented by changes in everyday practices that have emerged within capitalist political economies

In the remainder of this introductory chapter, I discuss the fundamental concepts and imperatives of capitalism, give a brief overview of its historical formation and geographical expansion and introduce the ways that life in capitalist societies has led to the formation of habits oriented to growth and individualism. In Chapter 2 I sketch out a theory of the everyday habits of capitalism, with its roots in important work on habit in the early and mid-twentieth century, when habit was one of the central concerns in social theory. I draw on my own and other recent research that builds on the habit theories of Pierrre Bourdieu, Marcel Mauss and others, and apply it to an understanding of the relationship between capitalism and everyday energy consumption. In Chapter 3, I provide examples of expansive energy-using habits in the domains of thermal comfort, cleaning, food and transport. I reflect on how these habits might be broken and reformed at lower energy intensities. Having explored the synergies between the political economy of growth and consumption habits, in Chapter 4 I discuss mainstream approaches to low carbon transformation. These can be classified under the broad heading of green economy, in which the transformation to low energy and low carbon is delegated to markets and technical efficiency. I will argue that mainstream green economy approaches are relatively toothless and that much more radical policies and practices will be needed to engender a significant shift in entrenched habits. In Chapter 5 I reflect on needed changes in low carbon governance, which will entail a reassessment of fundamental principles of expansive economics, including growth, free markets and the diminished role of government in strategic energy and carbon reduction policies. I will be arguing that there is a need for a comprehensive transformation of the capitalist system, targeting its central features of economic expansion and individual ownership. In Chapter 6, I draw attention to examples of the growing numbers of communities who are attempting to put social and environmental goals ahead of economic growth, private ownership and consumerism, and to reduce their community and household energy use and carbon emissions while maintaining or improving wellbeing and life quality. I will also give attention to non-localized collaborations to reduce consumption through sharing and extending the lifetime of goods through reuse and exchange. In the concluding chapter, I explore the power of denialists, many of them related to or financed by the fossil fuel industry, to inhibit low carbon transformation and the recent signs that denialists are losing their political legitimacy. I also explore the low carbon potential represented by the Nordic soft versions of capitalism and the European efforts to make the economy circular. I conclude by returning to the argument that low carbon will not be achieved without breaking and reforming the habits of capitalism and suggest a new public policy focus to begin the formidable task of making this happen.

The habits of capitalism would not be an issue if capitalism as an organizing system had not had severe and unrelenting consequences for both the global and local ecosystems as well as the related problems of maldistribution of wealth and the concentration of political power in the hands of energy capitalists. In the wake of the instability of the global economy in the 2000s, the global financial crisis and subsequent recession, much of the discussion and critique of capitalist political economy has centred on the volatility and opaqueness of financial markets; the fragmenting of work and resulting underemployment; and in general on how to 'avoid another economic meltdown in the future' (Pryor 2010: 1). While the central focus of this book will be on capitalism's consequences for climate change, I regard these broader environmental and social consequences of capitalist political economy to be related in ways that will be addressed in the coming chapters. As I will argue, a transformation towards a more just distribution of economic wealth will have positive benefits for the environment.

We have known about the association between energy use, emissions of CO_2 from the burning of fossil fuels and climate perturbation since the 1980s. The emissions of CO_2 are the main source of the overheating of land and oceans, accompanied by abnormal climate events such as storms, flooding and heat waves. The main source of carbon emissions results from the conversion of fossil fuels – petroleum, coal, natural gas – into products and energy, either directly into motive power such as that which fuels automobiles and other forms of transport, or through burning them and converting them into electricity in thermal power plants. Electricity in turn enables the running of a multitude of technologies in industries, commercial buildings and homes. Increasing CO_2 emissions are directly linked to the increasing volume and amounts of energy we use to heat and cool buildings, fuel transport, provide clean bodies and much more. Carbon and energy are the 'lifeblood' (Huber 2013) of capitalist economy and society, yet the consequences of this dependence in the form of carbon emissions and other environmental problems are severe and are getting worse with every molecule of CO_2 emitted.

The main within-capitalism solution for reducing energy-related climate emissions is the replacement of fossil fuels with other energy sources that do not emit carbon, such as sun, wind, geothermal and nuclear power. As I have argued in several recent publications, the transformation to renewable energies, while important, will not happen fast enough, nor assume a large enough share of global energy production over the next couple of centuries to make a significant dent in carbon reductions (Wilhite 2012). In the highest carbon-emitting country, the USA, even the latest and most ambitious plan for reducing carbon emissions assumes that 70 percent of primary energy use in 2030 will be from fossil fuels (compared to 72 percent in 1990) and 15 percent from renewable energy sources (CSE 2015). The most lucrative alternative source of energy, solar, has disadvantages relative to fossil fuels regarding storage and production at scale which limit its uses in industrial production and large-scale electricity production (Altvater 2007). In Chapter 4 I will argue that mainstream 'green' economy approaches to reducing carbon are overoptimistic in their assumptions about the capacity for renewable energies to achieve urgently needed rapid and significant decreases in carbon emissions. I will also argue that the consumption of the things that use energy will have to be reduced in numbers and size, including reductions in the sizes of the houses in which we live and in the energy used to produce essential in-home services such as thermal comfort, clean bodies, food and transport. Achieving these reductions will demand challenging the cornerstones of capitalist political economy – growth, individualism and consumerism – and reforming the habits that this economic system have fostered.

The authors of several recent books argue that capitalism in its current form would never have come about without the availability of fossil fuels (oil, coal and natural gas) and the development of technologies and industries dedicated to their extraction and conversion to useful energy. Concerning coal, as Naomi Klein (2014: 175) puts it, 'coal was the black ink in which the story of modern capitalism was written'. At the beginning of the twenty-first century, coal reserves remain plentiful, their extraction and conversion cheap and their environmental consequences extensive, not only in the form of climate perturbation but also in the form of local pollution from the emissions of sulfur, nitrogen and particulates. Mathew Huber (2013) argues convincingly that oil has been crucial to the sustenance of capitalism. He makes the case that the USA is addicted to oil, and 'that the problem of oil addiction is about not only our material relation with energy resources but also how energized practices spawn particular forms of thinking and feeling about politics' (2013: xi). This insight harkens back to the work of anthropologist Leslie White and his insight that 'modern capitalist (twentieth century) society was a fuel society to its core; its achievements were fundamentally predicated on fuel consumption such that rampant consumption had become archetypal throughout its culture' (cited in Boyer 2014: 311). As Altvater puts it 'In comparison with other energy sources, fossil energy fulfils almost perfectly the requirements of the capitalist process of accumulation. It fits into capitalism's societal relation to nature' (2007: 41).

The USA is the country in the world with the purest form of capitalism and the highest level of per capita energy use and carbon emissions. Capitalism has infiltrated the political economies of Europe and in recent decades has spread to seemingly unlikely places like India, Vietnam and China (see contributions to Hansen and Wethal 2015b). Capitalism frames the practices of global institutions such as the World Bank and International Monetary Fund (IMF), and over recent decades is borne by transnational corporations operating in and through expanding global markets. It has a solid grip on national governance in many parts of the world and influences the everyday lives of an increasing share of global householders.

The pillars of capitalism

In order to set the stage for the discussion of capitalism and climate emissions in the coming chapters, in this section I will briefly discuss the central elements of capitalism as a societally organizing system, drawing heavily on recent analyses by Piketty (2014), Harvey (2014) and Klein (2014). This will include a sketch of historical developments in capitalist-oriented political economies, giving special emphasis to the post-1970s neo-liberal trends in which increasing consumption has become a backbone of capitalist economic development.

David Harvey broadly defines capitalism as any social formation in which 'processes of capital circulation and accumulation are hegemonic and dominant in providing and shaping the material, social and intellectual bases for social life' (2014: 17). The pillars of capitalism are economic growth, individual ownership, marketization, product differentiation and product turnover. Capitalists are the owners of capital, which Thomas Piketty (2014: 46) defines as 'the sum total of nonhuman assets that can be owned and exchanged on some market'. He writes that the goal of capitalists is 'to increase productivity, efficiency and profit rates, and to create new and, if possible, ever more productive product lines' (2014: 92). Capital generates income in the form of rents, dividends, profits and wages. The owners of capital benefit from the former (rents, dividends and profits), while their labourers are allocated the latter (wages). A society organized according to capitalist principles is thus divided into two factions, those who make income from capital (wealth) and those who make income from selling their labour to capital (work). Piketty and others demonstrate that in capitalist-organized societies, the proportion of wealth diverted to the owners of capital relative to labourers has increased over the past century, accelerating in recent decades. In other words, the rich are getting richer. Globally, the wealthiest 2 percent of the global population now owns 50 percent of the wealth. In the USA, the wealthiest 22 percent of the population owns 80 percent of the wealth and the bottom 20 percent only 1 percent of the wealth. Samir Amin refers to this unjust distribution as a consensual *apartheid* involving the submission of a large segment of the society to the domination of capital (2003). In Chapter 4, I will explore the reasons for this submissiveness and lack of mobilization for change grounded in either social or environmental concerns.

Capital can lie latent in nature, in the form of land, forests or ocean ecosystems, or result from human activity, such as buildings, roads, electricity systems and water delivery systems. Nature and its constituents become capital when they are assigned exchange value in markets (become commodified) and sold. Through a capitalist lens, nature's use values as represented by the water we drink and the foods we gather become replaced with exchange values in market-driven economies. In the words of Altvater (2007: 39), 'Nature is remarkably productive...but it is not *value productive*, because it produces no commodities to be sold on the market. There is no market in nature. The market and commodities are social and economic constructs, not a natural heritage, even if neoliberal economists assume otherwise.' The transformation of nature into commodities is the source of a number of environmental problems. First, in a growth economy, the tempo of commodification and extraction is faster than nature's tempo of regeneration. Second, certain natural 'products' are linked to other organisms in forests and ocean ecosystems; their extraction can disturb a wide range of these organisms and even lead to ecosystem failure. Third, natural systems are sinks for certain forms of pollution that emanate from the production and consumption of energy and other materials. This leads to problems that are not adequately accounted for in market pricing. Capitalization not only strips nature of its intrinsic value, but also alters it, generating what economists refer to as 'externalities' of capitalist activities in the form of costs borne by society (pollution and ecosystem perturbation) that are not attributed to the extractor's or producer's accounting. Climate gas emissions are a classic example of this problem. Emissions of CO_2 and other climate gases such as methane are affecting tropospheric and oceanic systems in ways that will lead to substantial changes to life on earth. A central argument in this book is that a mild retrofit of the growth-oriented capitalist system will have a minimal impact on climate emissions and do little to ameliorate its consequences.

Capital is both a store of value and a factor in production. But capital degrades and gets worn out over time (at least the built variety) and capitalism depends not only on the search for new products but the replacement of worn-out capital. 'Before wages are distributed or dividends paid and before genuinely new investments are made, worn-out capital must be replaced or repaired. If this is not done, wealth is lost, resulting in negative income for the owners' (Piketty 2014: 43). Furthermore, capitalists, in the form of either individuals or corporate entities, must compete for market shares of commodities if they are to survive and flourish. As Marx observed in volume I of *Capital*, capital accumulation is crucial to the survival of both the capitalists and the capitalist system. This encourages 'Accumulation for the sake of accumulation, production for the sake of production' (1976: 742). The drive to accumulate drives in turn a search for new products, markets, production techniques and raw material sources in nature (Castree 2008). The success of capitalism relies on new forms of commodification, the renewal of old capital and surplus generation. Each of these interferes in natural ecosystems both through extraction and pollution. Ironically, in national economic accounting, cleaning up pollution and treating the health problems to which it contributes is counted positively in measures of the common index used to measure economic growth, the Gross Domestic Product (GDP) (Brown and Carver 2009: 11).

Private ownership and individualized private property rights form other pillars of capitalism. Harvey (2005: 160) writes that private property 'is a necessary condition and construction (in capitalism) in the sense that neither exchange value nor money could operate in the way it does without this legal infrastructure (supporting private ownership)'. Economic growth and development rely heavily on formalized property systems because capitalization not only allows for growth: it imposes it. Furthermore, increasingly, property ownership in modern capitalism is dependent on indebtedness. For households in capitalist societies, credit and loans enable the purchase and use of a series of increasingly bigger houses over the course of a household's life cycle as well as new appliances and furnishings that are purchased, discarded and replaced at a rapid tempo. According to Cross (2000), debt-based consumption did not come into being until the end of the nineteenth century, but it increased rapidly in the early 20th century. By 1924, in the USA 70 percent of new cars were bought on credit, as were 70 percent of furniture, 75 percent of radios, 80 percent of phonographs and 80 percent of household appliances. After the stock market crash of 1929, many home owners in the USA went into default on their loans. The Homeowners Loan Corporation was established in 1933, a government agency dedicated to help families avoid foreclosure. In 1934, the Federal Housing Administration was established, which guaranteed private loans and the standardization of 10 percent down payments and 30-year paybacks. From the 1950s, in the USA household debt steadily increased, quadrupling between 1980 and 2010 (Klein 2014: 75). Total debt grew from about 1.5 times the US national output in the early 1980s to nearly 3.5 in 2007. The financial sector's share of US profits increased from about 15 percent in the early 1950s to almost 50 percent in 2001 (Faulkner 2013: 291). Since 1970 in the USA, average incomes have declined, but purchasing power has increased due to credit- and debt-financed consumption.

Altvater (2007) argues that credit is crucial to the growth of the most recent phase of capitalism. Governments, companies and households all accumulate debt in order to expand, and the repayment of debts is in turn dependent on expansion. In his book on the intimate relationship between oil and capitalism, Huber (2013) argues that debt consumption and other characteristics of the ways national economy is conducted have been absorbed into the ways that middle-class households conduct their household economics. The combination of post-war neo-liberalism and the rapid growth in single-family housing have contributed to the transformation of home life into what Huber refers to as a mini-capitalist, private sphere in which the accumulation of money and goods is made possible through debt financing. 'Putting property at the center of social reproduction is central to the multiplication of entrepreneurial subjectivities… The cultural politics of entrepreneurial life is only made common sense through access to credit and the accumulation of debt, where one's own working life is forever entangled in a constant process of paying down debt' (2013: 23). The most recent phase of credit-based, temporal expansion has allowed national and household economies to grow through mortgaging the future, permitting the continued exploitation of material resources in the form of land, fuels and minerals, as well as driving continued increases in pollution and carbon emissions (Weltzner 2011).

In capitalist societies, individual ownership has been celebrated as one of the ultimate aims of development by national governments, commercial businesses and household consumers. Habituation to individual ownership and is one of the greatest challenges to a low carbon transformation. From an environmental perspective, the individualized ownership and use of shelter (home); household appliances (such as heating and cooling systems, refrigerators, cooking appliances, washing machines and clothes driers); and cars demand high volumes of energy to run them as well as energy needed to produce them and either recycle or dispose of them. In Chapter 6, I will argue that increased sharing and collaboration is crucial to breaking high energy habits and reforming them at lower energy intensities.

The roots of capitalism and the imperative to grow

The roots of the various forms of capitalism found in the world today can be traced back to the 15th and 16th centuries. Global trade expanded rapidly, allowing a growing class of merchants to accumulate massive amounts of wealth. This was accompanied by a growth in the influence of intellectuals who exalted reason and argued that societal progress was dependent on scientific knowledge. As Navarez (2013: 24), writes, 'the world of ideas (mind, ego, the subject) was radically sundered from the world of matter (the body, the external world, the object)'. Descartes convinced the intellectuals of his time that to be human is to partake from two radically different natures: the mind, the 'captain of the ship', and the body, a 'corpse' or a 'machine'. By the eighteenth century, European societies were 'intoxicated by the newly discovered omnipotence of "reason", which was expected to explain passions, politics and deities' (Andrusz 1999: 11). This separation of mind and body influenced the organization of the economy and reinforced the class distinction between owners (brains) and workers (bodies). A further distinction was made between wage labour in the formal economy and labour not associated with wages, such as housework, which 'was left behind and conceptualized as traditional labour; that is, non-modern' (Mignolo 2011: 300). Thus economic and social progress was associated with salaried workers who accepted their role as wage takers. As I will argue in Chapter 2, the body and embodied knowledge need to be restored to the epistemologies of consumption (human–technology interactions) and applied to the policies of low energy and low carbon.

While notions of economic prosperity continued to be influenced by the notion of scientific and technological progress in the nineteenth century, Darwin's theory of evolution gave societal progress an internal logic that associated historical stages with ever greater achievement. This was consistent with Hegel's philosophy of the historical expansion of spirit and in the vision of capitalist accumulation (Miller 1987). As Piketty (2014: 9) writes

> In a world where capital was primarily industrial (machinery, plants, etc.) rather than landed property...there was no limit to the amount of capital

that could be accumulated. In fact, his (Marx's) principal conclusion about capitalism was what one might call the 'principle of infinite accumulation', that is, the inexorable tendency for capital to accumulate and become concentrated in ever fewer hands, with no natural limit to the process.

Marx's analysis of capitalism contended that the progressive accumulation of capital and power into the hands of a few would lead to its own destruction and be followed by a new stage of collectivism. So far with a few exceptions, the main experiments in collectivist economy on a large scale – the Soviet Union and the countries of Eastern Europe – eventually imploded. After the collapse of the Soviet Union and communist satellites in the 1990s, there have been no challenges on a grand scale to the association of growth, private ownership and capital accumulation with societal progress, a healthy economy and improved conditions of living. Today, these associations 'pervade our political discourse, the writing of history, and the consciousness of ordinary people everywhere' (Hamilton 2003: 98).

In the words of Amin and Thrift (2004: x), in capitalist societies, the social and the economic 'are woven together in a single and inseparable fabric'. This has created 'a form of civilization that endows all of its members with a bio-graphical model that stipulates interminable, self-transcendent growth' (Weber cited in Weltzner 2011: 24). Growth and expansion in capitalist societies are sought after by politicians, capitalists, investors, employees and consumers. In the world of everyday business, any capitalist commercial enterprise is obliged to grow in order to secure profit generation and unless it grows, it has no chance of surviving in a competitive market or of producing dividends for shareholders (Ingham 2008). As Smith writes,

> Corporations have no choice but to grow. It is not 'subjective'. It is not just an 'obsession' or a 'spell'…shareholders are not looking for 'stasis'…so they drive their CEOs forward…Corporate CEOs do not have the freedom to choose not to grow or to subordinate profit-making to ecological concerns because they don't own their firms even though they may own substantial shares.
>
> (2010: 31, cited in Wilhite and Hansen 2015: 38)

According to Arndt (1978: 33), prior to 1950, there were no traces of economic growth as an objective in any national economy. He writes that the first official government pronouncement that favoured economic growth as a national policy objective was that of the US Council of Economic Advisors in 1949. In the single decade of the 1950s, growth became a paramount objective of national government policy in the US and European countries. In many domains of everyday life, growth has seeped into the habitus of everyday lives, leading to energy-using habits that are disposed towards expansion, a central point in this book to be developed in Chapters 2 and 3. As the tentacles of capitalism have extended from the USA and Europe to other parts of the world, the culture of capitalism has followed in its wake. Capitalism has sustained growth through geographic expansion of both labour and resources (colonialism, international trade, transnational corporatism) and through temporal expansion (credit-based production and consumption). Capitalism has taken on different forms and has taken root in differing cultural and national contexts. Capitalism does not homogenize culture everywhere, in fact research shows that changes in the cultural fabric in differing national and cultural settings are sometimes unique and even surprising (Wilhite 2008). Nonetheless, a common thread in emerging capitalist cultures is the goal of rapid economic growth, increased productivity and an increasing tempo of consumption.

The ascendance of neo-liberal capitalism

In his analysis of the ebb and flow of historical trends in capitalism, Michael Burawoy (2014) relates how, due to the devastation of the great depression, Keynesian capitalism was embraced by President Franklin Roosevelt as a response to the depressed US economy of the 1930s and 1940s. This version of capitalism emphasizes a role for the public governance of, and public investments in the economy, as well as public stewardship of strategic resources such as energy and water. Keynesian principles remained present in the post-World War II US political economy in the governments of Kennedy and Johnson in the 1960s, but in the 1970s there was an ascendance of market fundamentalism and no-government governance. Under Ronald Reagan in the USA and Margaret Thatcher in the UK, state intervention was increasingly seen as an anathema to a well-functioning economy, disturbing the effectiveness of 'market signals' on matters of investment, resource allocation and demand (Harvey 2005). The subsequent dominating version of capitalism has been termed neo-liberal capitalism. As Stuart Hall (2015) famously put it, the formula for this form of capitalism was a simple one: capital was to be free, and people were to be disciplined. The grip of neo-liberalism on governance in the past half century has weakened environmental governance and stepped up capitalism's assault on the environment.

Neo-liberal capitalism gained legitimacy when one of its strong intellectual proponents, Freidrich August von Hayek received the Nobel Prize in economics in 1974, followed by a second Nobel Prize two years later to another neo-liberal economist, Martin Friedman. Naomi Klein (2014) recounts how Friedman and his 'Chicago School', with the backing of the US government, became the acolytes of neo-liberalism in Latin America. Following the US-supported coup of Salvador Allende's left-leaning government in 1973, Chile became the site of a neo-liberal experiment. Friedman and his colleagues supported coup leader Augusto Pinochet's reconstruction of the Chilean economy. As a result, Chile privatized public assets, opened up natural resources to private and unregulated exploitation, privatized the social security system and facilitated foreign direct investment and free trade. The right of foreign companies to repatriate profits from their Chilean operations was guaranteed. Harvey writes that this experience lead to a form of U-turn globalization because it was to influence the direction of US and European political economies: 'for the first time, a brutal experiment carried out in the periphery became a model for the formulation of policies in the centre' (2005: 9). In the USA, Ronald Reagan put neo-liberal principles into practice in his presidential periods in the 1980s. Under Reagan, there was a massive deregulation of industries, a privatization of resources (water and energy) and dramatic reductions in corporate taxes and personal income tax rates. Tax rates for the highest income brackets were reduced from 70 percent at the beginning of Reagan's term to 28 percent at the end of his term. In 1979, the top 5 percent earned ten times more than the bottom 5 percent. In 1993 the difference was 25 fold. The new government of Margaret Thatcher in the United Kingdom in 1979 created a powerful pan-Atlantic neo-liberal axis. Thatcher privatized national industries, including the coal industry and the railways, broke the back of organized labour and reduced social welfare support. Both of these governments encouraged an increase in the casualization of labour and a redistribution of wealth from labour to capital (Faulkner 2013: 270).

International development organizations have been important agents in the global extension of neo-liberal capitalism. Beginning with the collapse of the Mexican economy in 1984, the IMF and the World Bank initiated a policy of providing huge loans and export credits in return for neo-liberal reforms. Conditions imposed by the IMF and World Bank – referred to as 'structural adjustment' – emphasized downsizing of government, maximizing market freedom and protecting private property rights: 'The IMF and the World Bank thereafter became centers for the propagation and enforcement of "free market fundamentalism" and "neoliberal orthodoxy"' (Harvey 2005: 29). In return for debt rescheduling, developing countries were required to implement institutional reforms, such as cuts in welfare expenditures, more flexible labour market laws, and the privatization of previously owned government industries. The World Bank was a zealous guardian of the growth imperative. Larry Summers, the chief economist of the World Bank, wrote in 1992 (quoted in Barry 2011: 129),

> There are no limits to the carrying capacity of the earth that are likely to bind any time in the foreseeable future. There isn't a risk of apocalypse due to global warming or anything else. The idea that we should put limits on growth because of some natural limit, is a profound error and one that, were it ever to prove influential, would have staggering social costs.

By 2000 the World Bank recognized the need to respond to criticism that it was not taking the environment seriously and to embrace the concept of 'sustainability'. In 2001, the World Bank president James D. Wolfensohn (World Bank 2000: 29) wrote 'Growth in material well-being is a central element in advancing human welfare and reducing poverty...Sustaining (economic) growth over the long term therefore requires that such (environmental) problems be addressed integrally in current growth strategies and investment programs.' It is noteworthy that Wolfensohn reversed the usual meaning of sustainability in which economic development should be adjusted to the environmental limits. For Wolfensohn, the environment is to be protected so that economic growth can be sustained. As I will develop in Chapter 4, the World Bank and the IMF have been instrumental in creating and applying conditions to loans and export credits in development projects that require the freeing up of markets, privatization of the commons, downsizing governments and growing the economy. As thoroughly documented by Harvey (2012: 28) in his research on globalizing capitalism, the World Bank continues to make elliptical references to the need to do something about social and environmental consequences of their project proposals, but there is little follow-up action. The goal continues to be to impose 'the usual nostrums of neoliberal economics', getting government out of social and environmental planning, opening land and ecosystems for commercial enterprise and other forms of commodification and encouraging entrepreneurial activities that support the overall goal of growing the economy. According to an analysis of World Bank activities by Banerjee (2007), their overall effect has been the strengthening of local elites, increasing social inequality and accelerated environmental deterioration. In the absence of a strong governmental imposition of incentives and penalties, low carbon transformation and ecosystem restoration are delegated to a market that is indifferent to its environmental consequences.

By the end of the first decade of the twenty-first century, all of the Organisation for Economic Co-operation and Development (OECD) economies were capitalist and increasingly adapting neo-liberal principles: 'all have predominantly private ownership of the means of production; all have relatively free competition…and all have relatively few restrictions on consumers' (Pryor 2010: 15). Victor (2008) refers to a report by the OECD in 2005 to demonstrate the continued strength of economic growth as an OECD and national political economic goal. In the forward to the report entitled 'Economic policy reforms: Going for Growth', the OECD Secretary General writes: 'As policy makers and others grapple with the challenges posed by the increasing interdependence of our economies, growth has to be at the top of our agenda' (OECD 2005: 4, cited in Victor 2008: 18). As I will explore in Chapter 4, growth continues to be at the heart of new, green economic initiatives in the OECD countries, including green economy and circular economy.

Capitalism and the 'emerging economies'

The fall of the Soviet Union in 1989 and the integration of China and India into the global economy occurred at the apex of the global wave of neo-liberal capitalism. In subsequent years, Brazil, Mexico and other populous countries have 'emerged' and integrated into the global capitalist economy. In a recently published book edited by Hansen and Wethal (2015a), the emerging economies of China, Vietnam, India, Brazil and other rapidly developing countries are analysed from the perspective of whether there are any indications of new models for environmentally sustainable development. Each of these countries is in the process of transitioning from a state-driven socialist (or quasi-socialist in the case of India) economy to a mixed political economy that could be labelled 'market-oriented socialism'. Each of these has a goal of 'greening' their economy. The conclusion by Hansen and Wethal is that these greening efforts generally follow the greening agendas of the OECD countries, which count on increased energy efficiency and renewable energies to do the work of reducing environmental impacts of growth:

> Despite the mainstreaming of sustainable development in development discourses, growth strategies pursued in emerging economies are resembling the cruder development thinking of the 1960s with economic growth taking the driver's seat (with little concern for equity or the environment)...Across all three regions (Asia, Africa and Latin America), we find strategies of 'green growth', 'green capitalism' or 'ecological modernisation' being adopted, based on the claim that the market can serve as a tool for confronting the challenges of sustainable development.
>
> (Hansen and Wethal 2015a: 269)

In China, market economics was embraced by Deng Xiaoping in 1978, setting the stage for phenomenally high growth rates over the ensuing decades, but the environmental costs have been enormous. China has opened for foreign investment and transnational corporations, as well as assuming the role of global manufacturer in a number of industries, including the environmentally problematic textile and automobile industries. The growth of the textile industry has skyrocketed due to China's cheap labour and weak environmental regulations. The low production cost of textiles and clothing for US and European clothing retailers has reduced the price of clothing dramatically worldwide and is contributing to what Kline (2014) describes as a 'disposable' clothing culture. Because about 70 percent of China's energy production is based on coal, the textile and other manufacturing industries are responsible for producing both CO_2 emissions and several forms of severe local pollution. China now has 20 of the 30 most polluted cities in the world, extensive water pollution, including 90 percent of urban ground water and 30 percent of rivers. In many parts of China, water is unsuitable for agricultural irrigation. In 2012 China's coal-based energy production was four times that of the USA and eight times that of Europe; with 20 percent of the world's population, China has a coal-based energy production equivalent to the rest of the world. China's carbon emissions have increased by 230 percent since 1990. Coal production is expected to increase by 50 percent by 2040, despite China's plans to develop and use renewable energy such as solar and wind. The renewable energy strategy is only making a small dent in the growth of energy use and CO_2 emissions because of China's rapid economic growth, based on increasing production for the global economy and increasing domestic consumption. Both the consumption of cars and household appliances are growing rapidly in China. The number of cars on the road tripled from around 5 million in 1990 to 18 million in 2013, and according to Smith (2015) the number of cars is expected to reach between 390 and

530 million by 2050. China's CO_2 emissions are growing faster than any country in the world and have recently surpassed the USA's emission levels.

The 'opening of India' to global capitalism from the mid-1980s to mid-1990s set the stage for rapid economic growth, reduced the role of government in the economy and increased the influence of transnational capital. One of the conclusions of my research in India on economic liberalization and the resulting growth in consumption is that the opening of markets and premiering of consumption have over three decades contributed to substantial changes in household habits and significant increases in energy use (Wilhite 2008). The liberalization broke with a 40-year post-independence history in India characterized by planned economy, redistributive policies and scepticism to Western consumerism. According to Chandhoke (2005), a strong government role was widely accepted by the influential industrialists of the 1950s. There was broad consensus that state control and the extension of development benefits to everyone 'were deeply interrelated' (2005: 1038). The policy of keeping the global capitalist economy at bay lasted until the 1980s, when slow economic growth and widespread poverty led to a serious debate on whether the planned economy should be abandoned and India's markets opened to the global economy. The erosion of the state-planned and production-oriented economy was accelerated after the fall of the Soviet Union in the late 1980s and India's geopolitical 'middle way' between the Western and Soviet blocks dissolved. In 1990, a Congress-led government was elected and its Minister of Finance, Manmohan Singh, announced a package of liberalizing reforms. Foreign investments were encouraged, import duties relaxed on a wide range of products, and transnational corporations were invited to directly invest in India or to engage in joint ventures with Indian companies. The government took an IMF loan of USD 2.8 billion, bringing with it demands for deep structural reforms, including downsizing the public sector, privatizing public enterprises and establishing conditions for freer markets (Corbridge et al. 2012). From the mid-1990s the Indian political economy increasingly took on board neo-liberal capitalist principles. At the level of everyday life, consumption of cars, air conditioners, household appliances and entertainment technologies increased dramatically and new energy-intensive habits began to form around comfort, transport, food consumption and entertainment. According to the contributions of Hansen and Wethal (2015b), similar liberalizing economic trends and growing middle-class consumption are evident in Vietnam, Brazil and other emerging economies.

Habituation to individualized consumption and growth

The opening of the Indian economy and subsequent increases in consumption reveal many of the same dynamics associated with the maturation of capitalism in the USA and Europe in the early and mid-twentieth century. In pre-World War II Western capitalism, production was regarded as the backbone of the economy. Social identities were associated with work. There were 'white-collar' and 'blue-collar' workers, related to the type of clothing typically worn by office workers and managers on the one hand, and labourers on the other. Raising one's social status was accomplished through moving up in the work hierarchy or changing to a higher status job. From the 1950s, the emerging middle classes in the USA and Europe began to be identified as (and assume the identity of) consumers. It can be said that the middle class became synonymous with the consumer class. According to Cross (2000: 51) from the mid-twentieth century, 'The future through consumption meant more than bigger and better or greater social status. It also suggested faster and faster change…Americans seemed to forget their old goal of rising up the ladder of professional success for the more obtainable objective of "buying a living" and "the expectation of material progress without end"'. The ascendance of neo-liberal capitalism has fostered an everyday life in the USA that 'mirrors the entrepreneurial logics of capital…based on privatized social reproduction, single-family housing, and automobility…a postwar social construction of life as composed of homes, cars and yards' (Huber 2013: xiv). Harvey (2014: 70) mirrors this point: 'The idea of a stable good life and of good living according to modest requirements is displaced by an insatiable desire for gaining more and yet more money power in order to command more and yet more consumer goods'.

According to Robbins (2004), the interweaving of consumption and capitalism resulted in what he defined as the 'culture of capitalism'. At its heart, this culture embraces 'a vision of the world designed to maximize production and consumption of goods' (Robbins 2004: 14). One cannot neglect the power of media and advertising in supporting this vision. In the USA, advertising began experimenting with messages and sharpening sales techniques in the early twentieth century. Cross writes that advertising revenues rose in the USA from USD 542 million in 1900 to 3.43 billion in 1929. In 1931, advertising constituted 65 percent of the content in women's magazines (Cross 2000: 34). Radio advertising in the 1930s was 'massive', especially effective after the invention of the 'soap opera', devised by soap manufacturers as a platform for selling soap and beauty products, and adapted by television in the 1950s with great success. Soap operas are permeated with advertising breaks that are tolerated by viewers who are hooked on following the storyline through episode after episode and commercial break after commercial break. By the mid-1990s there were about 6,000 commercials aired per week on US television. According to Cross, in 1991, 15 minutes of every hour was devoted to commercials.

Harvey's assessment is that twentieth-century capitalism has had 'pervasive effects on ways of thought to the point where it has become incorporated into the common-sense way many of us interpret, live in, and understand the world…If successful, this conceptual apparatus becomes so embedded in common sense as to be taken for granted and not open to question' (2005: 3). This is consistent with Gramsci's repeated point in his writings that capitalism's common sense is embedded in 'habitual social practice' and that 'good sense' would only come about by reflexively engaging with and renegotiating capitalism's imperatives (Ekers et al. 2009: 289). As I will develop in Chapters 2 and 3, capitalism's 'common sense' of growth, speed, convenience and comfort is driving the formation of habits that make a heavy demand on energy and materials to heat and/or cool bigger houses, power household appliances and provide motive power for bigger and faster cars. This 'common sense' persists in spite of a growing body of evidence that after a certain point of economic development, increased wealth has little impact on people's feelings of wellbeing (Guillen-Royo and Wilhite 2015). As Massey writes, pursuing growth 'is a chimera since, while growth may occur, all the evidence is that our levels of satisfaction with our lives remain obstinately static. We should be thinking of "the economy" not in terms of natural force and intervention but in terms of a whole variety of social relations that need some kind of coordination' (2013: 15).

In the coming chapters, I will argue that post-World War II capitalism has succeeded because its ideology, institutions and incentives have fostered practices that over time have embodied and habituated expansive consumption. The growing critique of economic growth from a sustainability and carbon-reduction perspective does not adequately address the challenge of transforming everyday habits. This is one of the important explanations for why efforts to reduce climate consequences and reduce energy use have only been marginally effective. Proposals for 'greening' capitalism – with a strong dose of market regulation, technological innovation and managerial perfection – have left intact the power of economic growth both in political economy and household consumption. Variations on the theme of green economics treat economy 'as if it has broken away from human society and assumed a life of its own' (Hamilton 2003: 120). I will outline why green economics as they are now constituted are not robust enough to engage with habits of growth or to generate significant reductions in energy use and carbon emissions. Mainstream theories and policies on energy and carbon reduction lack a focus on energy-using habits and an epistemology for dealing with them. New theoretical perspectives will be needed that examine the synergies between the collective and individual contributions to the habits of capitalism. In the next chapter I will lay out a theory of habit, arguing that it can provide a conceptual frame that acknowledges deeply held collective and individual dispositions for high energy consumption and provide insights on how low carbon policy can engage with high energy habits.

References

Altvater, Elmer. 2007. The Social and Natural Environment of Fossil Capitalism. *Social Register* 43: 37–59.

Amin, Ash and Nigel Thrift. 2004. Introduction. In Ash Amin and Nigel Thrift (eds), *The Blackwell Cultural Economy Reader*. Oxford: Blackwell Publishing.

Amin, Samir. 2003. *The Liberal Virus: Permanent War and the Americanization of the World*. New York: Pluto Press.

Andrusz, George. 1999. *The Co-operative Alternative in Europe: The Case of Housing*. Aldershot: Ashgate Publishing.

Arndt, H. W. 1978. *The Rise and Fall of Economic Growth*. Melbourne: Longam Cheshire.

Banerjee, Subhabrata Bobby. 2007. *Corporate Social Responsibility: The Good, the Bad and the Ugly*. Cheltenham: Edward Elgar Publishing.

Barry, John. 2011. Climate Change: The 'Cancer Stage of Capitalism' and the Return of the Limits to Growth. In Mark Pelling, David Manuel-Navarette and M. R. Redcliff (eds), *Climate Change and the Crisis of Capitalism*. London: Routledge, pp. 129–143.

Blundorn, Ingolfur and Ian Welsh. 2007. Eco-politics beyond the Paradigm of Sustainability: A Conceptual Framework and Research Agenda. *Environmental Politics* 16(2): 185–205.

Boyer, Dominc. 2014. Energopower: An Introduction. *Anthropological Quarterly* 87(2): 309–334.

Brown, Peter and Geoffrey Carver. 2009. *Right Relationship: Building a Whole Earth Economy*. San Francisco: Berrett-Koehler Publishers.

Burawoy, Micheal. 2014. Marxism after Polanyi. In Michelle Williams and Vishwas Satgar (eds), Marxisms in the 21st Century: Crisis, Critique and Struggle. Cape Town: Wits University Press.

Castree, Noel. 2008. Neoliberalising Nature: The Logics of Deregulation and Reregulation. *Environment and Planning* 40: 131–152.

Chandhoke, N. 2005. 'Seeing' the State in India. *Economic and Political Weekly* 11(12 March): 1033–1039.

Corbridge, S., J. Harriss and C. Jeffrey. 2012. *India Today: Economy, Politics and Society*. Cambridge: Polity.

Cross, Gary. 2000. *An All-Consuming Century: Why Commercialism Won in Modern America*. New York: Colombia University Press.

CSE. 2015. Assessing US Climate Action Plan. Report by the Centre for Science and Environment, Delhi. Available at http://www.cse.org. Accessed 17 October 2015.

EEA. 2015. Trends and Projections in Europe 2015: Tracking Progress towards Europe's Climate and Energy Targets. European Environmental Agency Report 4/2015. Available at http://www.eea.europa.eu/publications/trends-and-projections-in-europe-2015. Accessed 24 October 2015.

Ekers, Michael, Alex Loftus and Geoff Mann. 2009. Gramsci Lives! *Geoforum* 40: 289–291.

Faulkner, Neil. 2013. *A Marxist History of the World: From Neanderthals to Neoliberals*. New York: Palgrave.

Guillen-Royo, Monica and Harold Wilhite. 2015. Wellbeing and Sustainable Consumption. In W. Glatzer, W. (ed.), *Global Handbook of Well-being and Quality of Life*. Frankfurt: Springer.

Hall, Stuart. 2015. The Neo-liberal Revolution. In Sally Davison and Katherine Harris (eds), *The Neo-liberal Crisis*. London: Lawrence and Wishart, pp. 37–56.

Hamilton, Clive. 2003. *Growth Fetish*. London: Pluto Press.

Hansen, Arve and Ulrike Wethal. 2015a. Global Sustainability and the Rise of the South: Development Patterns and Emerging Challenges. In Arve Hansen and Ulrikke Wethal (eds), *Emerging Economies and Challenges to Sustainability*. London: Routledge, pp. 263–274.

Hansen, Arve and Ulrikke Wethal (eds). 2015b. *Emerging Economies and Challenges to Sustainability*. London: Routledge.

Harvey, David. 2005. *A Brief History of Neoliberalism*. Oxford: Oxford University Press.

Harvey, David. 2012. *Rebel Cities: From the Right to the City to the Urban Revolution*. London: Verso.

Harvey, David. 2014. *Seventeen Contradictions and the End of Capitalism*. Oxford and New York: Oxford University Press.

Huber, Mathew T. 2013. *Lifeblood: Oil, Freedom and the Forces of Capital*. Minneapolis: University of Minnesota Press.

Ingham, G. 2008. *Capitalism*. Cambridge: Polity Press.

IPCC. 2014. Climate Change 2014: Impacts, Adaptation, and Vulnerability. Available at http://www.ipcc.ch/report/ar5/wg2/. Accessed 20 September 2015.

Jackson, Tim. 2009. *Prosperity without Growth: Economics for a Finite Planet*. London and Washington, DC: Earthscan.

Klein, Naomi. 2014. *This Changes Everything: Capitalism vs. the Climate*. New York: Simon and Shuster.

Lynas, Mark. 2007. *Six Degrees: Our Future on a Hotter Planet*. London: Harper Collins.

Marx, Karl. 1976. *Capital, Vol. 1*, translated by Ben Fowkes. Harmondsworth: Penguin.

Massey, Doreen. 2013. Vocabularies of the Economy. *Soundings*. Available at http://www.open.ac.uk/researchcentres/osrc/files/osrc/Vocabularies%20of%20the%20economy_FINAL.pdf. Accessed 16 June 2015.

Mignolo, Walter D. 2011. *The Darker Side of Western Modernity: Global Futures, Decolonial Options*. Durham, NC and London: Duke University Press.

Miller, Daniel. 1987. *Material Culture and Mass Consumption*. Oxford: Blackwell.

Navarez, Rafael F. 2013. *Embodied Collective Memory: The Making and Unmaking of Human Nature*. Lanham, MD: University Press of America.

Patel, Raj. 2009. *The Value of Nothing: How to Reshape Market Society and Redefine Democracy*. New York: Picador.

Piketty, Thomas. 2014. *Capital in the Twenty-First Century*. Cambridge, MA: Belknap Press of Harvard University Press.

Prugh, Thomas, Robert Cosntanza and Herman Daly. 2000. *The Local Politics of Global Sustianability*. Washington, DC: Island Press.

Pryor, Fredric. 2010. *Capitalism Reassessed*. Cambridge: Cambridge University Press.

Robbins, Richard. 2004. *Global Problems and the Culture of Capitalism*. Boston: Allyn and Bacon.

Smith, Richard. 2010. Beyond Growth or beyond Capitalism? *Real-World Economics Review* 53: 28–42.

Smith, Richard. 2015. China's Communist-Capitalist Ecological Apocalypse. Available at www.truth-out.org/news/31478-china-s-communist-ecological-apocolypse. Accessed 23 June 2015.

Trusel, L. K., K. E. Frey, S. B. Das, K. B. Karnauskas, P. K. Munneke, E. van Meijgaarda and M. R. van den Broeke. 2015. Divergent Trajectories of Antarctic Surface Melt under Two Twenty-First-Century Climate Scenarios. *Nature Geoscience*. Available at http://www.nature.com/ngeo/journal/vaop/ncurrent/full/ngeo2563.html. Accessed 13 October 2015.

Victor, Peter A. 2008. *Managing without Growth: Slower by Design, Not Disaster*. Cheltenham and Northampton, MA: Edward Elgar.

WCED. 1987. *Report of the World Commission on Environment and Development: Our Common Future*. Oxford: Oxford University Press.

Weltzner, Harald. 2011. *Mental Infrastructures: How Growth Entered the World and Our Souls*. Berlin: Heinrich-Boll-Stiftung.

Wilhite, Harold. 2008. *Consumption and the Transformation of Everyday Life: A View from South India*. Basingstoke and New York: Palgrave Macmillan.

Wilhite, Harold. 2012. The Energy Dilemma. In K. Bjørkdahl and K. B. Nielsen (eds), *Development and the Environment: Practices, Theories, Policies*. Oslo: Universitetsforlaget, pp. 81–99.

Wilhite, Harold and Arve Hansen. 2015. Reflections on the Meta-practice of Capitalism and Its Capacity for Sustaining a Low Energy Transformation. In Marie-Christine Zélem and Christophe Beslay (eds), *Sociologie de l'énergie. Gouvernance et pratiques sociales*. Paris: CNRS Editions, pp 35–40.

World Bank. 2000. *Summary Proceedings, Annual Meeting 2000*. Washington, DC: World Bank.

WWI. 2013. *Is Sustainability Still Possible? State of the World 2013*. New York: Island Press.

2   A theory of habits

Theories of low carbon transformation have not come to grips with the relationship between capitalist political economies, with their emphasis on growth, private ownership and acceleration of consumption (product turnover), and the formation of everyday habits dependent on high and expanding amounts of materials and energy. My ambitious aim in this chapter is to develop a theory of habit that encompasses the interconnectedness of household habits and the political economy of capitalism. This conceptualization differs significantly from mainstream theories in low carbon and low energy research, which tend to treat political economy and everyday consumption as separate and distinct. My argument is that in the mature capitalist societies, many of the energy-dependent practices that give pleasure, provide comfort and deliver convenience, such as those associated with transport, shelter and entertainment, have formed tacit, collectively embedded associations with private ownership, expansion and speed, and that these in turn are bound up in high energy habits. A theory of habit has the potential to capture the collective and individual contributions to expansion of energy demand in capitalist societies, and the materialities deposited by capitalist development which are in turn structuring continued expansion. The political economy of capitalism embeds the seeds of growth, speed and individual ownership in everyday habits. The resulting capitalist culture disposes expansion in the form of bigger houses, more energy-intensive home cooling and heating, washing and food storage systems within the house and an increase in faster, energy-demanding individualized transport systems in urban geographies.

In this chapter I will sketch out a theory of habit, drawing on early twentieth-century work on habit, as well as recent theoretical applications to the understanding of consumption and energy savings. The discussion will involve debates on the place of mind and body in theories of action, as well as the agency of collective memory, social relations and material structures in everyday actions. In Chapter 3 I will give examples of high energy habits that have emerged in capitalist political economies, giving attention to the synergies between societal and household habits. I begin with a discussion of mainstream theories of energy consumption and savings which conceptualize consumption as individual-driven and reduce low energy policy to the provision of efficient technologies to rational economic actors.

Mainstream theories of household energy consumption and savings

The field of research concerned with theorizing energy consumption and promoting energy savings had its genesis in the wake of the 'oil shocks' of the 1970s. The theories and politics of energy savings in the intervening years have been dominated by theories of rational choice and technical positivism. Economic rationality is assumed to be 'the driving seat of human action' (Hodgson 2004: 653). This ignores much of what is important in consumption and in social life: consumers have differentiated knowledge, are embedded in social relations and perform their everyday practices in historically deposited material settings. Many economists are aware of the reductions and limitations of their rational choice models, but they have nonetheless dominated the theories and policies of energy consumption and savings and made it difficult to get purchase for other perspectives that attempt to draw in the complex interplay between social, economic and material relations in consumption. Anthropologist Laura Nader writes that a 'culture of energy experts' consisting mainly of economists and technologists has promulgated a view of consumption that ignores 'the very wide range of choices of life-styles that is available in any plausible energy future' (2014, quoted in Boyer 2014: 314). What consumers want is stripped of considerations of what they wanted in the past and how this has been deposited in material structures and socio-technical systems. Through buying into the cognitive centred, rational, individualist conceptualization of consumption, energy research and policy has reduced energy savings to a matter of changing consumer's minds and attitudes, mainly through various forms of information and price incentives.

Critiques of these rationalist and behaviouralist conceptualizations of energy consumption have mainly come from sociology and social anthropology (see Wilhite et al. 1996; Wilhite et al. 2000; Nader 2004; the contributions to Strauss et al. 2013); however, they have also been critiqued within economics. Norwegian Nobel Prize winner Trygve Haavelmo wrote that 'Existing theories of behavior are not good enough…We start by studying the behavior of the individual under various conditions of choice…We then try to construct a model of the economic society in its totality by a so-called process of aggregation' (1989). More recently, Thomas Piketty wrote in his historically grounded analysis of capitalism (2014: 32):

> To put it bluntly, the discipline of economics has yet to get over its childish passion for mathematics and for purely theoretical and often highly ideological speculation, at the expense of historical research and collaboration with the other social sciences…This obsession…is an easy way of acquiring the appearance of scientificity without having to answer the far more complex questions posed by the world we live in…they (economists) must set aside their contempt for other disciplines and their absurd claim to greater scientific legitimacy, despite the fact that they know almost nothing about anything… The truth is that economics should never have sought to divorce itself from the other social sciences and can advance only in conjunction with them.

Institutional economist Geoffrey Hodgson (1997: 664) echoes this point, writing that economics needs to make an effort to take on board the social contributions to behaviour.

> The prime goal (of economics) is not to explain individual behavior but the intended and unintended outcomes of the interacting behaviors of many agents…(and) the social character of cognition, enquiry and learning…In order to gain knowledge of the world we require prior clues and cognitive frames that are provided in part through social interaction with others.

Behavioural economics acknowledges that some behaviours are 'non-rational' and categorizes them as habitual (Kahneman 2003). Yet, what is meant by habitual is undeveloped, posed as a kind of residual category of action that does not respond to rational signals. This conceptualization has led to low energy policies that attempt to 'nudge' consumer choices in the desired direction (towards buying a given product) by altering the cognitive context such as rearranging the display of products in a retail store so that the desired product draws the attention of the consumer (Jones 1999). I agree with Hodgson's scepticism to this view of behaviouralist amendment to rational choice theory: 'While it is a major improvement on the neoclassical paradigm, the behaviouralist approach neglects the social character of individual decision-making and also lacks a theory of the origin and adoption of rules and habits themselves' (1997: 678). In other words, perspectives on habit from within behaviouralist economics do not attempt to explain the sources and contributors to habits, and as such do not provide the basis for a robust theory of change.

Social practice theory

Frustration with the explanatory weakness of technical and economic accounts of consumption have fostered an interest in theories that give attention to social relations, the particularities of place (culture) and the influence of technology and materiality. The theories of Veblen (1899) and Bourdieu (1984) on the use of consumption as a means to achieve social mobility have been influential in demonstrating the need for incorporating a social perspective. This line of thinking was applied and developed by Schor (1992; 2010) to her studies on class, conspicuous consumerism and 'downshifting' in the USA. Shove and Warde directed attention to mundane and inconspicuous consumption inside the home and its nesting in broader regimes of social norms, technologies and infrastructures (Shove and Warde 2002). In recent years there has been a surge of interest in the application of social practice theory and science of technology studies (STS) to routine consumption. Developments in these two theoretical domains are important to the theory of habit I develop in this chapter. Social practice theory emphasizes the importance of three forms of knowledge that are brought to bear in routine actions: cognitive, experiential and material. STS puts emphasis on the ways that technologies and materialities, once designed and integrated into practices, influence action.

Social practice theory has its roots in the work of Bourdieu (1977; 1998) and his concept of habitus, defined as a domain of dispositions for action, created and perpetuated through the repeated performance of actions in a given social and cultural space. Bourdieu proposed that these dispositions influence subsequent performances of the same action. Over the past two decades, social practice theory has been developed and applied to theories of consumption (Schatzki 1996; Reckwitz 2002; Warde 2005; Shove et al. 2012; Sahakian and Wilhite 2014). A widely cited practice theorist, Andreas Reckwitz, defines a practice as 'a routinized type of behavior which consists of several elements, interconnected to one another: forms of bodily activities, forms of mental activities, "things" and their use, a background knowledge in the form of understanding, know-how, states of emotion and motivational knowledge' (2002: 249, cited in Warde 2005).

This practice approach moves the focus from cognitive and rationalist theories of action to embrace a theory of agency in which past experiences and the things with which the individual interacts are regarded as important to current and future actions. Theories of social practice give weight to the importance of tacit knowledge (otherwise conceived as experiential knowledge, know-how or dispositions) in human actions and to the contribution of social relations, collective norms and materialities to knowledge formation. Dispositions for future actions are created through past social interactions in places which are governed by formal rules and regulations, informal rules (cultural practices) and take place in material settings which in turn are agentive in practices. A theory of social practice distributes agency in consumption between cultural, social and material contributions to action (Wilhite 2008b).

From practice to habit

Theories of practice and habit are grounded in similar epistemological traditions. In the words of Shove, practices are 'entrenched practices that are recurrently and relatively consistently reproduced' (Shove 2012: 101). This 'entrenchment' can be due to deep cultural learning, heavy material constraints and by discursive narratives, such as those associating growth with progress and well-being. My argument is that life in capitalist societies is immersed in an interlocking set of narratives, materialities and incentives that has embedded the seeds of growth and accumulation in many of the practices of everyday lives A theory of habits draws attention to the synergies between the collective and individual contributions to the embodiment of growth, private ownership and rapid turnover of goods (buy and dispose). In this section I return to the genesis of habit theory in the early twentieth century and explore its development and importance in several academic disciplines, giving most attention to the sociology of habit as developed in the work of Marcel Mauss and Pierre Bourdieu.

This synergetic relationship between the collective and the individual was important in the social theory of the early twentieth century. A theory of habit was regarded by influential social theorists in several academic disciplines as an important theoretical construct for explaining human action. From differing disciplinary platforms, Thomas Veblen, James Dewey, William James and, later, Marcel Mauss, Pierre Bourdieu and others viewed the concept of habit as a lens through which to theorize social patterns and practices. There were different nuances in their theories of habit, but many important similarities: common to all was the proposition that lived experience in a place forms dispositions for both thought and action, and that these affect future actions. There were also different views as to whether habits were properties of mind or of body. The habit theorists from economy and psychology tended to assign habits to mind, influenced by the legacy of Descartes and his association of 'being' with 'thinking'. In this view, the theorizing of actions like consumption was 'beyond body, above history and geography' (Mignolo 2011: 203). Many of the early habit theorists conceived of a layered mind, consisting of a conscious, reflexive layer and a 'non-conscious' layer, arguing that the latter was important in habit formation. Mauss and Bourdieu expanded the focus from mind to body, emphasizing the importance of the embodiment of knowledge to the formation of habits. Their view was that bodies and minds both participated in actions and that the body/mind was a repository of non-reflexive knowledge brought to bear in actions involving everything from body-close actions such as sleeping to more complex actions involving more than one individual or in which tools and technologies were engaged or deployed.

Verplanken and Aarts (1999) trace interest in habit in psychology to the writings of William James in the 1890s. William James' crucial insight was that past experience contributes knowledge that is important to the performance of future actions. As paraphrased by MacMullan, James believed that experience 'lives in and through us, so much so that it usually moves us without our conscious permission, indeed, sometimes without even our notice' (2013: 235). James and other leading psychologists of the time proposed that experience manifests itself in the form of learning and memory systems that operate separately from intentions. Many forms for human action were said to operate on 'minimal awareness', 'lack of conscious intention' and 'lack of control'. Fredreich Hayek (1948) drew on these perspectives in his mid-century writings on 'inarticulate knowledge', the basis for what he referred to as 'techniques of thought', knowledge that was brought to bear in action but which could not be articulated by the performer. Michael Polanyi (1969) picked up on Hayek's theory of the inarticulate and termed it tacit knowledge, paraphrased by Oguz as 'unexpressed mastery that does not allude to any kind of articulate knowledge' (2010: 147). Polanyi illustrates this with an example of how a blind mind uses a stick: 'when a blind man first faces a stick, he attempts to understand it. He learns how to use it, tries to master it. After learning how to use a stick, he no longer pays attention to it. It becomes an extension of his bodily existence' (cited in Oguz 2010: 147). Despite this reference to body, Polanyi and other psychologists tend to situate habits in the mind. This is captured in the definition of Verplanken and Aarts: a habit is 'a cognitive mind set, i.e., an enduring cognitive orientation that makes an individual less attentive to new information and courses of action, and thus contributes to the maintenance of habitual behavior' (1999: 103). This cognitive view of habit set the stage for the emphasis in psychology on cognitive instruments such as attitudinal and motivational information as levers for changing habits (Kok et al. 2011).

Noteworthy from the perspective of the dominant neo-classical rationalist theories in economics today, habit had a central place in economics in the early twentieth century. Hodgson, reviewing historical changes in economics, argues that early 'institutional' economists such as Thorstein Veblen, Mark Baldwin, William Thomas and Florian Znaniecki rejected the view that human action is driven by rational, calculating agents and embraced a concept of habit as a means of drawing attention to the role of 'institutions' on action. Institutions for these economists resembled 'social structures' important in sociological and anthropological theories of action at the time, such as social relations, norms, symbols and rules. Institutions were seen to frame and condition behaviours, but 'they were neither reducible to nor ontologically equivalent to them' (Hodgson 1997: 681). Early institutional economics was interested in the 'mechanisms by which habits and rules build up to social routines and institutions...as well as the feedback loop by which institutions help in turn to reinforce particular habits and rules'(1997: 681). Habits 'provided a highly sophisticated understanding of the relationship between individual agents and social structures, and provided a meta-theoretical framework for understanding economic change' (Hodgson 2004: 7).

Early institutional economists such as Veblen and Dewey shared with psychologists of the time the interest in experiential knowledge and how it creates dispositions for future actions. Dewey (1922: 42, cited in Hodgson 2004: 652) wrote that 'The essence of habit is an acquired predisposition to ways or modes of response'. Rephrased by Hodgson (2004: 652), for Veblen and Dewey, 'Habits are submerged repertoires of potential behaviour...Habit is a *propensity* to behave in a particular way in a particular class of situations. The propensities or dispositions created by experience and repetitive action were seen as important to cognition and decision making' (Hodgson 2004: 169). According to Hodgson (2004: 170), this interest in disposition would later be put aside in economics because 'If habits affect behavior then it is wrongly feared that reason and belief will be dethroned...However from a pragmatist perspective, reasons and beliefs themselves depend upon habits of thought' (1997: 666). A theory of habit is antithetical to rational choice and theories based on utility maximization and on rule-compliance, the core assumptions of late twentieth-century economics.

As Hodgeson points out, early institutional economists differ not only from neo-classical and behavioural economics that would emerge later, but also from the 'new' institutional economics that emerged in the mid-twentieth century, which equates institutions not with epistemologically defined social structures but with real organizations. In other words, there has been a turn in institutional economics away from an application of sociological concepts to the study of human action and towards the development of organizational theory and an analysis of organizations.

Interest in habit as a sociological concept waned in every branch of economics at mid-century. However, interest in experiential knowledge, disposition and habit lived on in social anthropology and sociology in the work of Marcel Mauss (1973) and Pierre Bourdieu (1977). Mauss preceded Bourdieu in coining the term *habitus* to capture the domain of knowledge on which body and mind draw in performing countless actions in the course of a day. Mauss proposed that lived experience embodies knowledge related to the ways we dress, eat, clean, organize space and use time, highly relevant for understanding the ways we cool and heat our homes, prepare and consume foods, wash and clothe our bodies and transport ourselves from one place to another.

Mauss made it his project to emphasize the importance of the body in action. He coined the term 'body techniques' (1973), perhaps in order to draw attention to his emphasis on body in contrast to Hayek's emphasis on mind in his 'techniques of thought'. Both Mauss and Hayek acknowledge a form for knowledge that influences action yet operates below the level of conscious reflection; however, Mauss emphasized the role of cultural learning in the embodying of knowledge that then becomes agentive in many kinds of actions including body-near actions such as sleeping, walking and talking, as well as other more complex actions involving the use of tools and technologies such as eating, cleaning (ourselves and our close environments) and keeping warm. As summarized by Navarez, Mauss' perspectives on body techniques and habit 'suggests that history and society, social ranks included, were inscribed upon our bodies and were thus daily performed by us' (2013: 11).

Mauss pointed out how another related form of embodiment occurs through purposive training in sport, dance and other forms of body-crucial activities such as typing. An important point is that learning these activities involves both reflexivity and bodily engagement, but a good dancer, swimmer or typist is one in which embodied skills are brought to bear in performances. Waquant's (1995) study of boxers emphasized how both embodiment and reflexivity are crucial to the development of boxing skills. As Crossley (2013: 293) writes about Mauss' views of body and action, body techniques 'are forms of knowledge and understanding which operate at a pre-reflective, pre-conceptual level, consisting entirely in an embodied mastery of particular types of situation and a capacity to do certain sorts of things...but this knowledge cannot be articulated in discourse'. The importance of cultural difference in embodied knowledge was brought out in a study of household energy consumption in Japan and Norway, which revealed significant cross-cultural differences in body-near practices such as bathing, keeping warm and home lighting (Wilhite et al. 1996).

Bourdieu refined and developed the concept of experiential knowledge – what he later referred to as practical knowledge (1998) – over the course of his academic career. He used the term disposition much in the same way as early habit theorists, as a structuring of future actions by knowledge generated through past experiences. He used the term *habitus* to mean a field of dispositions which engages with the 'presence of the past' (1998: 304) in forming and embodying knowledge. *Habitus* can therefore be understood as embodied history. To use

Bourdieu's terminology, 'The body politic implants in me a *habitus* by immersing me in an array of tangible movements and routines that effectively 'deposit' an orientation within' (quoted in Smith 2013: 95). In one passage in his Outline of a Theory of Practice, Bourdieu (1977: 94) writes about the importance of embodiment to the formation of habits:

> Dress, bearing, physical and verbal manners are aspects of the fundamental principles of an arbitrary nature of culture. The principles em-bodied in this way are placed beyond the grasp of consciousness, and hence cannot be touched by voluntary deliberate transformation, cannot even be made explicit: nothing seems more ineffable, more incommunicable, more inimitable, and, therefore, more precious, than the values given body, made by the transubstantiation achieved by the hidden persuasion of an implicit pedagogy, capable of instilling a whole cosmology, an ethic, a metaphysic, a political philosophy, through injunctions as insignificant as 'stand up straight' or 'don't hold your knife in your left hand'.

For both Mauss and Bourdieu, the body is a repository of past experiences, both individual and collective, and as such, the body is thus not only the site of action, but also of dispositions for future actions. The sources of agency in embodied actions are not always transparent to the subject. The body predisposes actions that are accomplished without conscious direction, but also allows purposive actions (such as typing, sports, dance) to be carried out without conscious intervention. Heating, cooling, switching lighting on and off, closing doors and showering are examples of energy-dependent actions in which bodies and bodily knowledge are important in the formation of habits.

From the discussion of habits thus far it should be evident that the concepts of experiential knowledge, disposition and habit have had important places in theories of knowledge and action and actually were regarded as central to social theory in the early twentieth century. Habit has maintained a place in psychology and behavioural economics, but theories are cognitive and mind-oriented, divesting bodies from explanations of action. This view is exemplified in this passage by psychologists Verplanken and Wood in which they define habits 'as a form for automaticity in responding that develops as people repeat actions in stable circumstances' (2006: 96). Wood, Tam and Guerrero Witt (2005: 932) give attention to the 'triggering' of action through repetition: 'When people practice action, they develop associations in memory between the actions and aspects of the context in which it typically occurs. With sufficient repetition in stable contexts, behavior comes to be triggered relatively automatically by these features of the performance context'. In anthropology and sociology, the interest in habit waned in the mid-twentieth century but has been revived and applied to consumption over the past decade (strongly influenced by the work of Alan Warde and Dale Southerton at the University of Manchester, see Warde and Southerton 2012). Shared by habit theorists is the notion that habit draws on collective and individual experience. Life in a social world (culture) populated by natural and human-made artefacts leads to both tacit knowledge and inter-pretive skills (cognition). Social theorists from psychology and economy tend to either ignore the body or to regard the results of its interactions with the world as properties of the mind. Recent research in sociology and anthropology draws attention to the role of the collapsed mind-body in remembering and deploying knowledge in human actions.

Materiality and habits

In my view neither the early work on habit nor the recent revival of interest in habit give sufficient attention to the contribution of material structures and technologies to forming and sustaining habits. In several publications over the past decade I have addressed why materiality should be given a stronger place in the theory of habit (Wilhite 2012; Wallenborn and Wilhite 2014; Wilhite 2015). An acknowledgement of the role of the material is important from a low carbon transformation perspective because those of us living in capitalist societies have inherited a material world which was built with little or no concern for the environment. The structures, infrastructures and technologies that have become central to life over the past century in houses, cities and nations have been shaped with an indifference to their environmental consequences. The materialities of modernity (Latour 1991) have set the stage for habituation to expansive con-sumption. I agree with Sennett when he writes that theories of society and materiality 'have failed to come to grips with the technologies it has created' (2012: 278). Efforts to reshape habits in a less energy-intensive direction will have to address the inertia in the built environments – cities, houses, home appliances, roads, electricity and water delivery systems – shaped by capitalist expansion, private ownership and speed.

In this section I will address two related aspects of materiality relevant to habit formation: material scripting of action and the displacement of know-how from bodies to technologies. Material scripting has been one of the main con-ceptual concerns of the field of studies that calls itself science of technology studies (STS), yet there has not been a strong coupling of this line of research to theories of social practice and habit. Drawing on perspectives roughed out by Heidegger on technology agency, Bruno Latour, John Law, Wiebe Bijker and others have put together a theory of action which assigns agency in human actions to both the material and the human (see Bijker and Law 1992). The proponents of STS support the commonly accepted proposition in non-economic social science that humans use objects in both routine and sometimes unex-pected ways, but they also draw attention to the ways that this causality is reversed and material objects shape action. According to STS, those who design or shape the technology inscribe 'scripts' for its use that in turn shape the practices into which they are inserted. This shaping can be determinative; for example, a door determines how people enter and leave a room; persuasive, such as how a kitchen built with a space for a dishwasher invites the new occupants to buy and insert one; or more subtle in its influence such as how the persistent use of a washing machine affects perceptions of cleanliness and, in turn, frequency of washing. Applying this theory to energy and water using technologies, such as washing machines, showers and radiator-based heating systems, there is a deeper structuring of action that derives from the interlinked regime of materials and infrastructures in place to deliver water and electricity (Southerton et al. 2004). Once the regime of time-saving, convenient and comfort-delivering modern technologies is in place, it strongly influences the ways that thermal comfort, clean bodies, clean clothes, food and transport are practised. Take transport as an example: the twentieth-century city was designed for automotive transport. In urban landscapes, public transportation systems and cyclists were literally squeezed off of the roads. In some North American cities, sidewalks were eliminated to make more room for automobiles. In other words, urban materialities are strongly scripted for the car. Walking, cycling and using public transportation must overcome inconveniences, time delays and safety risks

Another example of a strongly scripted regime of technologies involves the house and the standard technologies and appliances within it. In the USA and Europe, where household appliances have, one after the other, become normalised in many household practices over the course of the twentieth century, there are many examples of how the changing structure of the house and the numbers of technologies in it are reshaping practices and locking people into habits that will be difficult to break and reform. In household activities such as cleaning clothes, preparing food, attending to the comfort levels in the house (heating and cooling), the technology contributions to action have intensified dramatically, as have the urban infrastructures that favour automobiles in practices related to commuting, shopping and accomplishing other tasks outside the home, such as transporting children to school and after-school activities. Technologies are taking over the work of bodies in many everyday practices. Virtually every routine household task involves the use of either a tool or energy-using technology. These tools and technologies can be viewed as extensions of the body (Wallenborn 2013). The use of tools such as brooms, mops, fans and kitchen devices in tasks such as sweeping, cleaning floors, adjusting ventilation and cooking relies on bodily action and body agency. In the case of technologies such as washing machines, tumble dryers, air conditioners and food processors, they need only be set in motion with the pushing of a button or twisting of a dial. Both work and agency are transferred from the body to the technology and this sets the stage for the formation of technology and energy-dependent habits.

Another significant transformation in everyday practice involves the cleaning of clothes and the notions of what it means to look clean. Of all of the modern household appliances, perhaps the appliance that saves the most time and physical work is the washing machine. When cleaning clothes 'by hand', the body is active in soaping, rinsing and beating out the dirt. In India, where washing by hand is still common, washing the equivalent of a single washing machine load can take up to two hours (Wilhite 2008a). A washing machine replaces washing, rinsing and beating with putting the clothing to be washed into the washing drum, adding detergent, setting a dial and pushing the start button. Cleaning is delegated to the machine, which takes over the process of adding water, controlling cleaning cycles, centrifuging the load and draining off the rinse water. Body actions are limited and the energy and water used opaque; thus body labour and time constraints are no longer factors in deciding how often to wash clothes.

In their research on how people use common household appliances in the USA, Pierce et al. (2010: 5) confirmed that for most people, clothes-washing decisions were tacit and habituated. In one representative answer to questions about washing routines, one of the respondents said she had 'always' done the wash by putting the clothes in the machine and turning the dial to setting '9'. When asked why, she responded '*I've been doing this for a long time. My mother told me to do that...I don't think "regular 9". Like, I've never said to myself, hmm: "regular nine", nine o'clock. I just know it goes to here* [demonstrating setting]. *I don't consciously think about the 9*'. When asked about the washing machine programme, another respondent replied '*I've also never ever, ever turned this dial to anything but here* [indicating 'normal' cycle]...*But yeah, as far as that goes, I have no idea at all as to what those things would do. I've never, ever not done this.*' When asked what it would take to change washing practices from using warm water for washing to using cold water wash cycles, another respondent answered '*I don't know...I guess, if they started making washing machines with only that option, because everything was alright with cold... They must be giving you these options for a reason. Now, I suppose if I bought a washing machine that only had a cold cycle on it, then that's what I'd do.*' The delegation work and know-how from body to washing machine is quite evident among these respondents, reflecting Hodgson's point that 'mechanical habits can remove important actions from the due exercise of deliberation and creative skill...While the very rigidity of habits is necessary to fix learning and fasten skills, such rigidity can often be disabling, particularly when faced with a new and complex problem' (1997: 676).

The sealing of the house into a comfort bubble

There is no more powerful demonstration of material agency in the formation of energy-intensive habits than in the transformation from buildings that are built for cooling using ventilation, shading and fans to those that seal off the inner climate of the house from the outside climate and pump in refrigerated air. This sealed comfort bubble has impacted on the ways people experience comfort, making the creation of comfort significantly more energy demanding. In the next chapter I will discuss how this building comfort bubble has expanded over the past half century, increasing the amount of energy needed to achieve air-conditioned comfort. The sealed house, coupled with central systems for mechanical cooling, heat and ventilation, limits the ability of occupants to regulate air flow in and out of the house and within the house, as well as to create different levels of cooling in different parts of the house. From a habit perspective, indoor climate control is transferred from active bodies to passive thermostat controls and smart meters, which as I will develop in the next chapter tend to be ignored, misunderstood and misused.

Shove and Wilhite (1999) relate how a typical house of the 1950s in the 'sun belt' in the USA was built with small windows on southern exposures, had trees and other natural shading where possible and was built with screened-in verandas that one could relax and dine on, and which provided a conduit for ventilation for the house. Living in these houses during peak summer heat required the active involvement of bodies in regulating comfort. This involved changing the weight of clothing depending on the time of day and location, moving the locus of socializing and eating with the movement of the sun, the positioning of floor fans and the opening and closing of doors and windows. From the 1960s, the arrival of room air conditioners led to moderate changes in these patterns; then the central air conditioning systems of the 1970s led to more drastic changes. By 1980, 27 percent of US households had central air conditioning and in 2009 this more than doubled to 63 percent (US Energy Information Administration 2012). As Shove et al. (2010) point out this precipitated a new concept of separate indoor and outdoor comfort in hot climates. Screened porches were glassed in and the default position of doors and windows changed from open to closed. The flow of people, food and socializing between living room and garden was restricted to the cool of the evening. Instead of regulating movement and clothing according to shading and the time of day, people developed clothing habits that were suitable for mechanically regulated cooling.

There have also been significant historical changes in home heating habits. Shove (2003) draws attention to the significant changes brought on by the transformation to central heating and systems. In Europe as late as the eighteenth century, the house had one or more heating sources, such as fireplaces and woodstoves. In rural areas, many farmers brought their farm animals into the house during the winter to protect them from the elements, but also in order to add their body heat to the indoor climate. As durable and effective building insulation became available, the animals were put back in the barn, but the home continued to be heated by point sources in Europe until well into the twentieth century and the arrival of the central heating system. From the early twentieth century, architects and engineers associated the future of home comfort in the sealed house with a mechanically supplied and automatically controlled comfort delivery system, providing indoor temperatures of 21°C year round for houses regardless of geographical location or time of the year (Shove and Moezzi 2002). The concepts and practices regarding building comfort have been strongly affected by a global association of engineers called the American Society of Heating, Refrigerating and Air-Conditioning Engineers (ASHRAE). Its interests and ambitions are evident in its mission statement (http://www.ashrae.org/about-ashrae):

ASHRAE, founded in 1894, is a global society advancing human well-being through sustainable technology for the built environment. The Society and its members focus on building systems, energy efficiency, indoor air quality, refrigeration and sustainability within the industry. Through research, standards writing, publishing and continuing education, ASHRAE shapes tomorrow's built environment today. ASHRAE was formed as the American Society of Heating, Refrigerating and Air-Conditioning Engineers by the merger in 1959 of American Society of Heating and Air-Conditioning Engineers (ASHAE) founded in 1894 and The American Society of Refrigerating Engineers (ASRE) founded in 1904.

Murphey (2006: 22) studied the impact of ASHRAE on building ventilation. She writes:

At its most economical and widely practiced in the nineteenth and early twentieth centuries, ventilation was simply opening windows. In contrast to this commonsense provision of fresh air, the emerging professional field of ventilation engineering solicited its business by arguing that only machines could reliably and precisely deliver fresh air in the volume and quality necessary to guarantee healthfulness...Bodies were standardizable entities – norms – requiring comfort. Buildings were boxes into which controllable comfort could be inserted.

This comfort vision, shared by building entrepreneurs, architects and engineers is nested soundly within the incentive structures and common sense of capitalism, involving deep-seated notions that technology could be used to conquer and control nature, as well as be a source of commodification, business generation, profit and growth. The ASHRAE vision strongly influenced government building regulations that required systems that could deliver mean radiant temperatures of 22°C, scripting a comfort norm at which the deliverers of air conditioning and heating systems must conform, and to which bodies adapted. ASHRAE standards are frequently referenced in national building codes and are commonly accepted standards for architects and engineers (Humphreys 1994). These standards have homogenized comfort norms and reduced flexibility in heating and cooling practices. There are a number of empirical studies of comfort perception in buildings that demonstrate that this 22 degree norm is arbitrary and far lower than people in either naturally cooled or air conditioned buildings are comfortable with. Comfort systems have been designed to provide 22°C in all microclimates and seasons, whereas people have been reported to be comfortable at a wide range of temperatures, from 6°C to 31°C (Nicol and Humphreys 2009). A comparative study set up by Busch (1992) in Thailand examined the subjective perceptions of comfort in two office buildings, one naturally ventilated and the other air conditioned. He found that workers in the naturally ventilated building were comfortable working in temperatures up to 31°C, while those in the air-conditioned building were comfortable in temperatures up to 28°C. Busch suggests that 'acclimatization' to air conditioning is responsible for the difference.

Japan is a good example of how flexibility in regulating heating and cooling has been reduced in step with the standardization of building designs and materials over the past 40 years. In the 1990s, when point heating was still predominant, the average indoor temperature in Tokyo homes was about 17°C (Wilhite et al. 1996). Only certain spaces in the home were heated, such as under and around the dining room table and bathrooms. Buildings over the intervening period have been designed for central space heaters that heat the house to a 22°C standard. This contributed to an increase in average indoor winter temperatures to about 21.5°C in 2012. The changes in the creation of home comfort in the warm summers are equally dramatic. Japan went from no air conditioning in homes in 1960 to virtually 100 percent air conditioning in 1990. This resulted in a decrease in indoor summer temperatures and an elimination of flexibility in cooling practices (Wilhite et al. 1997).

The material scripts behind home heating and cooling technologies, supported by government regulations and standards and inscribed by designers and engineers, are nested within a capitalist economy that premiers competition, profit and energy using technologies and is either indifferent to or actively promotes increasing energy consumption. Once in place, the house and its comfort technologies decrease people's capacity for developing creative strategies to satisfy their own comfort needs. Moving into a dwelling built for air conditioning severely restricts the capacity to achieve cooling comfort without it (Wilhite 2009). In the words of Prins (1992: 255), air conditioning has conditioned bodies 'to hate the heat' and to construct the geographies of everyday life within comfort-sealed environments (houses, cars, workplaces and shopping areas) (Wilhite 2009). In Chapter 3 I will explore how this materially structured comfort transformation, nested within the expanding bubble of capitalism, is spreading to other parts of Asia. The building designs, materials, construction techniques and supporting regulations spread to Japan in the 1950s and 1960s and into China, Indian and Vietnam over the past three decades.

Conclusion

My aim in this chapter has been to develop a theory of habit that captures the contributions of capitalist development, manifested in regulations, standards and materialities, to the formation of high energy habits in homes. In con-solidating and developing a theory of habit, despite differences in vocabulary as well as in ontology, such as whether dispositions for action rest in the mind, body or mind-body, shared by habit theorists across academic disciplines is the notion that habit draws on knowledge that has both societal and individual sources. The review of the early psychological approaches from William James and John Dewey reveals that habits were regarded by them as 'social fulcrums' that connected the individual to society, otherwise theorized as 'social flywheels that bind together social relations and positions...Any effort to change or reform social relations must address the social habits that keep us tethered at least as much as, if not more than, the conscious and explicit ideas and arguments that seek to shore up these patterns of human relation'(MacMullen's 2013: 238). Bourdieu emphasized in all of his writings about habit that it has a collective element that is inherited through cultural learning and modified in the interaction between individuals and their social worlds. These collectively embedded dispositions resemble what Connerton (1989) refers to as collective memory. Navarez (2013:182) claims that important aspects of collective memory are embodied and are active in cultural reproduction. He writes that 'The body and memory…are depositories and crucibles of historical meaning, whose potentialities, though born in nature and framed by it, are largely realized through culture…collective pasts become sedimented in individual and social memories, in individual and "social bodies"…social beings embody, vivify and enact their historical time and social place'.

In Western, capitalist political economies, many of the practices that give pleasure, provide comfort and deliver convenience, such as those associated with transport, shelter (householding), entertainment and speed, have collectively embedded associations with expansion, individual ownership and commodification, whether measured in terms of bigger houses, accelerated lifestyles and more appliances. These associations are embodied and instrumental in the formation of habits that demand large amounts of energy. Even in a time when climate change and other environmental imperatives are inspiring new thinking on human–nature interactions, the political economy of capitalism and the material world that has been deposited by it over the past century are obstacles to the rapid transformation of stubborn habits. Buildings, transport infrastructures, food delivery systems and the household technologies with which people interact daily are scripted for the expansion of energy use. As I will exemplify in the coming chapters, the habits of capitalism, or habituation to capitalism if you will, involve a persistent escalation over generations and in personal and family histories of the material constituents of everyday practices, their energy intensity and their deliverables in terms of space heat and cooling, amounts of water consumed, kinds of food eaten, kilometres travelled and so on. The common sense of capitalism bears with it a vision of prosperity and the good life associated with material and energy expansion and this is accompanied by a regime of regulations, building standards and technologies which enforce this vision. The impact at the level of household has been habits oriented to expansion, the transformation of which will involve a much more ambitious low carbon policy exercise than those fostered in 'green economy' approaches (reviewed in Chapter 4).

A theory of habit brings bodies, tacit knowledge and material agency to the understanding of stability and change in important energy-using domains. It extends the analytical frame both backward and forward in time by acknowledging historically embedded experience and taking a long-term perspective on change. The challenge for a low energy, low carbon transformation is to enable habits that are grounded in sharing, collaboration, product longevity and the reinsertion of bodies into practices. This will demand a significant reorientation of current low carbon and low energy agendas in which the demand for goods is both disembodied and decontextualized from social and material worlds. It will involve a new genre of policies that enable experimentation and practical learning opportunities. Before exploring conventional green approaches to low carbon transformation in Chapter 4 and new perspectives in Chapters 5 and 6, I give examples in the next chapter of how the habits of capitalism have emerged and contributed to the escalation of demand for energy and an increase in carbon emissions.

References

Bijker, W. E. and Law, J. (eds). 1992. *Shaping Technology/Building Society: Studies in Sociotechnical Change*. Cambridge, MA: MIT Press.

Bourdieu, Pierre. 1977. *Outline of a Theory of Practice*. Cambridge: Cambridge University Press.

Bourdieu, Pierre. 1984. *Distinction: A Social Critique of the Judgement of Taste*. Cambridge, MA: Harvard University Press.

Bourdieu, Pierre. 1998. *Practical Reason*. Cambridge: Polity Press.

Boyer, Dominc. 2014. Energopower: An Introduction. *Anthropological Quarterly* 87(2): 309–334.

Busch, John F. 1992. A Tale of Two Populations: Thermal Comfort in Air-Conditioned and Naturally Ventilated Offices in Thailand. *Energy and Buildings* 18: 235–249.

Connerton, Paul. 1989. *How Societies Remember*. Cambridge: Cambridge University Press.

Crossley, Nick. 2013. Pierre Bourdieu's Habitus. In Tom Sparrow and Adam Hutchinson (eds), *A History of Habit: From Aristotle to Bourdieu*. Lanham, MD: Lexington Books, pp. 291–309.

Dewey, John. 1922. *Human Nature and Conduct: An Introduction to Social Psychology*. New York: Henry Holt and Company.

Haavelmo, Trygve. 1989. Econometrics and the Welfare State. Nobel prize lecture, 12 October, Oslo.

Hayek, F. A. 1948. The Socialist Calculation II: The State of the Debate. In F. A. Hayek (ed.), *Individualism and Economic Order*. Chicago: Chicago University Press, pp. 148–180.

Hodgson, Geoffry M. 1997. The Ubiquity of Habits and Rules. *Cambridge Journal of Economics* 21: 663–684.

Hodgson, Geoffry M. 2004. Reclaiming Habit for Institutional Economics. *Journal of Economic Psychology* 25: 651–660.

Humphreys, M. 1994. Field Studies and Climate Chamber Experiments in Comfort Research. In N. Oselund and M. Humphreys (eds), *Thermal Comfort: Past, Present and Future*. Waterford: Building Research Establishment, pp. 52–72.

Jones, B. D. 1999. Bounded Rationality. *Annual Review of Political Science* 2: 297–321.

Kahneman, D. 2003. A Perspective on Judgment and Choice: Mapping Bounded Rationality. *American Psychologist* 58(9): 697–720.

Kok, G., S. Hing Lo, G. Peters and R. Ruiter. 2011. Changing Energy-Related Behavior: An Intervention Mapping Approach. *Energy Policy* 39(9): 5280–5286.

Latour, Bruno. 1991. *We Have Never Been Modern*. Boston, MA: Harvard University Press.

MacMullan, Terrance. 2013. The Fly Wheel of Society: Habit and Social Meliorism in the Pragmatist Tradition. In Tom Sparrow and Adam Hutchinson (eds), *A History of Habit: From Aristotle to Bourdieu*. Lanham, MD: Lexington Books, pp. 229–255.

Mauss, Marcel. 1973 [1935]. Techniques of the Body, translated from the French by B. Brewster. *Economy and Society* 2: 70–88.

Mignolo, Walter D. 2011. *The Darker Side of Western Modernity: Global Futures, Decolonial Options*. Durham, NC and London: Duke University Press.

Murphey, Michelle. 2006. *Sick Building Syndrome and the Problem of Uncertainty: Environmental Politics, Technoscience and Women Workers*. Durham, NC and London: Duke University Press.

Nader, Laura. 2004. The Harder Path: Shifting Gears. *Anthropological Quarterly* 77(4): 771–791.

Navarez, Rafael F. 2013. *Embodied Collective Memory: The Making and Unmaking of Human Nature*. Lanham, MD: University Press of America.

Nicol, J. F. and M. A. Humphreys. 2009. New Standards of Comfort and Energy Use in Buildings. *Building Research and Information* 37(1): 68–73.

Oguz, Fuat. 2010. Hayek on Tacit Knowledge. *Journal of Institutional Economics* 6: 145–165.

Pierce, James, Diane Schiano and Eric Paulos. 2010. Home, Habits, and Energy: Examining Domestic Interactions and Energy Consumption. Proceedings, CHI 2010, 10–15 April, Atlanta, GA.

Piketty, Thomas. 2014. *Capital in the Twenty-First Century*. Cambridge, MA: Belknap Press of Harvard University Press.

Polyani, Michael. 1969. *Knowing and Being*. Chicago: University of Chicago Press.

Prins, Gwyn. 1992. On Condis and Coolth. *Energy and Buildings* 18: 251–258.

Reckwitz, A. 2002. Toward a Theory of Social Practices: A Development in Culturalist Theorizing. *European Journal of Social Theory* 5: 243–262.

Sahakian, Marlyne and Harold Wilhite. 2014. Making Practice Theory Practicable: Towards More Sustainable Forms of Consumption. *Journal of Consumer Culture* 14(1): 25–44.

Schatzki, Ted. 1996. *Social Practices: A Wittgensteinian Approach to Human Activity and the Social*. Cambridge: Cambridge University Press.

Schor, Juliet. 1992. *The Overworked American: The Unexpected Decline of Leisure*. New York: Basic Books.

Schor, Juliet. 2010. *Plentitude: The New Economics of True Wealth*. New York: Penguin Press.

Sennett, Richard. 2012. *Together: The Rituals, Pleasures and Politics of Cooperation*. New Haven, CT and London: Yale University Press.

Shove, Elizabeth. 2003. *Comfort, Cleanliness and Convenience*. Oxford and New York: Berg.

Shove, Elizabeth. 2012. Habits and Their Creatures. In Alan Warde and Dale Southerton (eds), *The Habits of Consumption: Studies across Disciplines in the Social Sciences*. Helsinki: Helsinki Collegium for Advanced Studies, pp. 100–112.

Shove, Elizabeth and Mithra Moezzi. 2002. *What Do Standards Standardize? Proceedings of the ACEEE 2002 Summer Study on Buildings*. Washington, DC: American Council for an Energy Efficient Economy.

Shove, Elizabeth and Alan Warde. 2002. Inconspicuous Consumption: The Sociology of Consumption, Lifestyles and the Environment. In Dulap, R., F. Buttel, P. Dickens and A. Gijswijt (eds), *Sociological Theory and the Environment: Classical Foundations, Contemporary Insights*. Plymouth: Rowman and Littlefield Publishers.

Shove, Elizabeth and Harold Wilhite. 1999. *Energy Policy: What It Forgot and What It Might Yet Recognize*. Proceedings from the ECEEE 1999 Summer Study on Energy Efficiency in Buildings. Paris: European Council for an Energy Efficient Economy.

Shove, Elizabeth, Heather Chappels, Loren Lutzenhiser and Bruce Hackett. 2010. Introduction. In Elizabeth Shove, Heather Chappels and Loren Lutzenhiser (eds), *Comfort in a Lower Carbon Society*. London: Routledge, pp. 1–16.

Shove, Elizabeth, Mika Pantzar and Matt Watson. 2012. *The Dynamics of Social Practices: Everyday Life and How It Changes*. London: Sage.

Smith, James K. A. 2013. *Imagining the Kingdom: How Worship Works*. Grand Rapids, MI: Baker Academic.

Southerton, D., H. Chappels and B. Van Vliet (eds). 2004. *Sustainable Consumption: The Implications of Changing Infrastructures of Provision*. Cheltenham: Edward Elgar.

Strauss, S., C. Rupp and T. Love (eds). 2013. *Cultures of Energy*. San Francisco: Left Coast Press.

US Energy Information Administration. 2012. *2012 Annual Energy Review*. Washington DC: US Department of Energy.

Veblen, T. 1899. *The Theory of the Leisure Class: An Economic Study of Institutions*. New York: Macmillan.

Verplanken, Bas and Henk Aarts. 1999. Habit, Attitude and Planned Behaviour: Is Habit an Empty Construct or an Interesting Case of Goal-Directed Automaticity? *European Review of Social Psychology* 10(1): 101–134.

Verplanken, Bas and Wendy Wood. 2006. Interventions to Break and Create Consumer Habits. *American Marketing Association* 25(1): 90–103.

WallenbornG. 2013. Extended Bodies and the Geometry of Practices. In E. Shove and N. Spurling (eds), *Sustainable Practices: Social Theory and Climate Change*. London: Routledge.

Wallenborn, G. and H. Wilhite. 2014. Rethinking Embodied Knowledge and Household Consumption. *Energy Research and Social Science* 1: 56–64.

Waquant, Loic. 1995. The Pugilist's Point of View: How Boxers Think and Feel about Their Trade. *Theory and Society* 24(4): 489–535.

Warde, Alan. 2005. Consumption and Theories of Practice. *Journal of Consumer Culture* 5: 131–153.

Warde, Alan and Dale Southerton (eds). 2012. The Habits of Consumption. *COLLeGIUM, Studies across Disciplines in the Humanities and Social Sciences* 12: 87–99.

Wilhite, H. 2008a. *Consumption and the Transformation of Everyday Life: A View from South India*. Basingstoke and New York: Palgrave Macmillan.

Wilhite, H. 2008b. New Thinking on the Agentive Relationship between End-Use Technologies and Energy Using Practices. *Journal of Energy Efficiency* 1(2): 121–130.

Wilhite, H. 2009. The Conditioning of Comfort. *Building Research and Information* 37(1): 84–88.

Wilhite, H. 2012. Towards a Better Accounting of the Roles of Body, Things and Routines in Consumption. In A. Warde and D. Southerton (eds), The Habits of Consumption. *COLLeGIUM, Studies across Disciplines in the Humanities and Social Sciences* 12: 87–99.

Wilhite, H. 2015. The Problem of Habits for a Sustainable Transformation. In K. V. Syse and M. Mueller (eds), *Good Life and Sustainability*. London: Routledge.

Wilhite, H., H. Nakagami, T. Masuda, Y. Yamaga and H. Haneda. 1996. A Cross-Cultural Analysis of Household Energy-Use Behavior in Japan and Norway. *Energy Policy* 24(9): 795–803.

Wilhite, H., H. Nakagami and C. Murakoshi. 1997. Changing Patterns of Air Conditioning Consumption in Japan. In P. Bertholdi, A. Ricci and B. Wajer (eds), *Energy Efficiency in Household Appliances*. Berlin: Springer.

Wilhite, H., E. Shove, L. Lutzenhiser and W. Kempton. 2000. The Legacy of Twenty Years of Demand Side Management: We Know More about Individual Behavior but next to Nothing about Demand. In E. Jochem, J. Stathaye and D. Bouille (eds), *Society, Behaviour and Climate Change Mitigation*. Dordrect: Luwer Academic Press.

Wood, Wendy, Leona Tam and Melissa Guerrero Witt. 2005. Changing Circumstances, Disrupting Habits. *Journal of Personality and Social Psychology* 88(6): 918–933.

3   The emergent high energy habits of capitalism

In this chapter I exemplify the ways in which the fundamental drives of capitalism to grow the economy, encourage individual ownership (and discourage sharing) and to commodify both comfort and cleanliness have fostered the emergence of high energy and carbon habits in important energy-using and carbon-emitting domains. As houses have expanded in size, home indoor climates sealed, the number of home appliances grown, bulk storage of food moved inside the home and a steady stream of new products produced and applied to practices of getting clean and making ourselves beautiful, energy-intensive habits have emerged. I will show these high energy habits are spreading to Asia and other rapidly developing countries.

Richard Robbins (2004) was one of the first to trace the emergence of expansive habits. He relates how in the USA, the consumption norms and habits of the late nineteenth century were characterized by moderation, thrift and frugality. These habits dissolved in the early twentieth century as the middle class grew wealthier and began to consume in ways that drew attention to their upwardly mobile progression through the social hierarchy (Veblen 1899, Bourdieu 1984). These expansive habits were to wither and frugality to reassert itself in the economic collapse that began with the stock market crash in 1929 and the ensuing 'Great Depression'. As Witkowski writes of the period (2010: 241), 'the prophecy of inevitable progress (that) had been so intimately equated with material growth and material expansion was invalidated'. The stock market crash, bank failures, massive unemployment and internal migration had profound emotional and psychological impacts. There was a return to consumption practices that were characterized by thrift and frugality. Goods of various kinds from clothing to cars should be used, patched up and maintained until they wore out. Many common household items were shared among families and it was common to share the house with relatives and rent bedrooms to strangers.

According to Witkowski, people from every segment of US society regarded the reasons for the economic collapse to be an unregulated economy. There was widespread support for Franklin Roosevelt's 'New Deal' which aimed at rerogulating the economy. The role of government was strengthened, not only as a regulator of markets but also as an investor and employer in a number of public projects. The federal income tax was created to finance government programmes. This government-led economy carried over into World War II, with public systems for product rationing and the reuse and recycling of a number of consumer goods (appliances, automobiles and tyres, fuel, some foods). This regulated economy that reached into many everyday practices was backed up with government-sponsored information campaigns that promoted the conservation of gasoline and tyres, the recycling of scrap metals and other materials, the planting of gardens and growing food at home, obeying price and ration controls and buying war bonds. Government agencies including the Office of War produced posters and advertisements for newspapers, radios and motion pictures encouraging thrift and frugal consumption. Schools, libraries, companies and volunteer groups contributed to this effort by disseminating posters conveying the need to share, conserve and moderate consumption. In the words of Witkowski (2010: 245), 'frugality received official sanction during World War II'. Fox (1975: 54) writes of the late 1940s, 'Perhaps never before, and certainly never since, were frugality appeals disseminated so widely in American society by so many and with such visual imagination and intensity. Consumer response was impressive: Americans recycled 538 million pounds of waste fats, 23 million tons of paper, and 800 million pounds of tin, while planting 50 million victory gardens'.

In the period following World War II this pervasive political economy of frugality was abandoned and replaced with an economy based on expansion and increased material consumption. In both the USA and Europe government, industry, media and banks all participated in economic expansion. The manufacturing industry grew rapidly in the USA and several European countries, driven by automobile production and the manufacture of household appliances. The expansion of energy production provided gasoline to fuel cars and electricity to power appliances. People worked longer in order to acquire and consume bigger houses, and women increasingly entered the workforce, making household appliances attractive to help them save time in the accomplishment of household tasks. In her book from 2003, Lizabeth Cohen describes this post-war period in the USA as a 'Consumer's republic' (Cohen 2003, see also Schor 1993). In the USA, residential energy consumption increased from 6 to 21.9 billion BTUs from 1950–2010, and this does not account for the energy used to manufacture products and components for both the houses themselves and the appliances and furnishings in them (US Energy Information Administration 2012). As I will exemplify in this chapter, high energy-using and carbon-emitting habits have formed which are deeply grounded in tacit ideas about prosperity and wellbeing, and manifested in a material world designed for high carbon living.

The house

From the 1950s, the sizes of houses have steadily increased in all of the Organisation for Economic Co-operation and Development (OECD) countries, as have the number and size of rooms (living rooms, bathrooms, bedrooms and kitchens), furnishings and household appliances. Figure 3.1 shows the increase in average house size in the USA from 1950 to 2010 and Figure 3.2 the growth in Norwegian house size and per capita house size from 1960 to 2000.

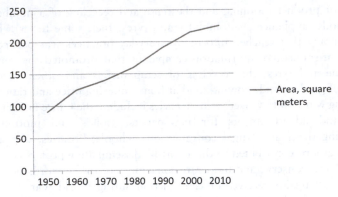

Figure 3.1 Growth in average house size in the USA 1950–2010
Source: National Association of Home Builders, Housing facts, figures and trends, March 2006, and US census bureau, 2010.

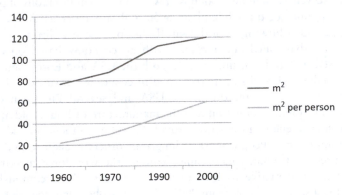

Figure 3.2 Growth in Norwegian house size 1960–2000
Source: Norwegian National Bureau of Statistics

As these two figures show, the size of houses doubled in the USA and increased by 50 percent in Norway. In the USA, expenditures on housing and household appliances increased by 33 percent from 1990 to 2014 and total carbon emissions from the residential sector increased by 28 percent over the same period (CSE 2015). In all of the OECD countries, the increase in amount of house space per person increased rapidly, and as Figure 3.2 shows, tripled in Norway. This can be partly explained by demographic trends such as ageing populations and increasing divorce rates, but this has been accompanied by a decline in the sharing of space with members of the extended family and a post-World War II view of the house as a strictly private sphere. Cross (2000: 61) writes how it was common in the USA in the early twentieth century for families to take 'boarders'. After the mid-century, the house became more like a 'moated castle' and a refuge from public life. In 2010, in the major cities in OECD countries 40–50 percent of dwellings (houses and apartments) had only one person living in them (Wilhite 2012). This increase in per capita dwelling space has brought with it an increase in demand for heating and cooling. In a study by the Energy Savings Trust (2009) in Great Britain, it was found that a three–four person household consumes about the same amount of energy for cooking and washing clothes as a house with only one person living in it and consumes only 18 percent more energy for dishwasher consumption. Single-person households were also found to use more electricity for lighting than families with three–four members. In a study of carbon footprints of US households, in which direct energy consumption is the largest component, Jones and Kammen (2011) found a non-linear relationship between the number of people living in the house and the carbon footprint. Single-person households in the study consumed a footprint that was more than half of that of four-people households.

Another development among rich and middle-class households in the USA and Europe has been the increase in the number of families with second homes. It is estimated that there are over 15 million second homes in the world, about one third of these in the USA and another third in France. These second homes extend the 'homescape' geographically (Appadurai 1996) and must be furnished with heating systems and appliances. In Norway, where 76 percent of house-holds own their house (or apartment), 19 percent also own a second house, usually located in the mountains or near the sea. A recent study by the Central Bureau of Statistics shows that the average size of the second home has grown over the past two decades and is now about the same size as first homes. There has been a change in the ways people furnish second homes in Norway in recent years. Whereas until the 1980s the second home (referred to as a cabin or 'hytte' in Norwegian) was regarded as a place for simple living – most cabins had no piped-in water or electricity – today the majority of cabins are furnished with many of the same household appliances of the principle residence (SSB 2014). Haugen (2008) studied household furnishings and energy practices in mountain cabins and found that the majority of people who own them replicate their first-home expectations for comfort and entertainment in their mountain cabin. Many of the owners maintain low heat and security lights year round, even though they may only use the cabin on occasional weekends or for a few weeks during holidays.

Within the expanding houses of the rich countries of the world over the past half century, the size of rooms has increased and new rooms have been added. In middle-class homes around the world, the average number of bathrooms and laundry rooms has increased. It has become more common for children to have their own individual bedrooms. There are indications that increases in house sizes in many OECD countries have recently begun to flatten out and in at least one country, the UK, decline, possibly due to the post-2009 economic recession but also because of physical limitations on space for new houses, particularly in urban areas. Many cities have placed limitations on building heights and in Europe cities have invoked regulations against continued urban sprawl in an effort to protect arable land and forests. Space limitations contribute to escalating prices for housing lots and provide an incentive to reduce the size of new houses. The result is a modest but interesting trend in small houses and micro-dwellings that is encouraging from an energy use and climate perspective. Still, even if this modest decline in the size of houses continues, the enormous increases over the past half century in the rich countries of the world have caused huge demands in the energy and materials needed to build and support life in them, and have fostered high energy habits that will be difficult to break and reform.

Energy-using technologies and appliances

The amounts and kinds of equipment and furnishings in the house have increased in step with increasing house size. From the beginning of the twentieth century, electrically driven devices became widely available and affordable. The electric fan, electric iron and cooking devices such as toasters, hotplates and waffle irons were all accessible by the turn of the twentieth century. After the electric plug was standardized and installed in homes in 1917, these and other electric appliances such as the vacuum cleaner and washing machine became more common. The refrigerator came on the market in the 1930s and by 1937, half of electrified homes had one (Cross 2000: 27). In one of the few comprehensive historical analyses of home electrical equipment, the Energy Savings Trust in Great Britain found that the number and kinds of electricity-using devices in homes in the United Kingdom have increased dramatically over the past 40 years (Energy Savings Trust 2009 and 2014). Entitled the 'Elephant in the Living Room', the report shows that the number of electrical appliances in UK homes tripled from the 1970s to 2002. The refrigerator/freezer and washing machine have become standard home appliances. Consumer electronics has contributed to a recent surge in home devices. In 1985 only 13 percent of UK households owned a home computer; ownership had increased to 75 percent of all households by 2009. In 2009, the average household owned 11 times the number of computers, printers, scanners and other computer-related devices than in 1970 and 3.5 times more than in 1990. Between 1970 and 2009 the electricity used for consumer electronics rose by more than 600 percent. While the average energy efficiency of home appliances of all kinds has increased by 2 percent per year since 1970, the electricity consumption attributable to domestic appliances has doubled. The study found that UK households owned 65 million electricity-using devices in 2012 and that in 2009, residential electricity use was responsible for 47 percent of CO_2 in the UK.

Looking towards the future, the Energy Savings Trust report predicts an increase in the ownership of tumble dryers, now owned by 45 percent of households, and dishwashers, now owned by 29 percent of households, and for all kinds of new computer electronics. Only a slight decrease is predicted in the electricity use for washing machines, cooking stoves and refrigerators over the coming decade, mainly because virtually every household has one. Nonetheless, the report warns against a 'fashion' for larger refrigerators that will use more electricity and encourage food waste. According to the report, UK households in 2012 threw away 480 pounds of food and drink every year. In Norway, which has seen a similar increase in refrigerator size to the UK, a study in 2013 found that Norwegian households discard about 225 pounds of food each year (Hanssen and Møller 2013). A US study showed that American households waste 40 percent of all edible food (Gunderson 2013). Much of this food waste can be attributed to the habit of shopping in bulk and using refrigerators as a kind of home mini-market that is oversized and encourages over-dimensioning food purchases and waste (Shove and Southerton 2000).

An interesting aspect of the Energy Savings Trust report from a perspective of expanding habits is that the Trust's 'ambitious' policy recommendations for reducing CO_2 emissions from household electric appliances includes efforts 'to understand consumer behaviour', but all of their suggested lines of inquiry relate to consumer response to efficiency standards, economic incentives and the wider use of energy efficiency labelling. The goal in this in much of government-sponsored research is to increase the efficiency of 'behaviour' through better information about efficiency and more efficient markets. The volume and numbers of energy-using things remain indifferent variables and policies oriented to transforming habits are virtually non-existent.

Thermal comfort

The expanding house contributes to an increase in the amount of energy needed to keep the house comfortable, whether it be cooling in the summer or heating in the winter. Policy aimed at reducing carbon emissions and decreasing energy use has put its weight behind regulations directed at increasing thermal efficiency of the building shell and/or the technical efficiency of the heating or cooling system. Neither the size of the space to be heated or cooled, nor increasing indoor temperatures have been targeted by energy savings policy. In places with cold climates, the combination of bigger houses, lower indoor temperatures in summer and higher indoor temperatures in winter are behind increases in the amount of energy to support home comfort. Efficiency-oriented countermeasures alone will not be sufficient to engender deep reductions in energy use. All these contributions to expanding space and increasing comfort demands will have to be addressed.

In Chapter 2, I used the example of air conditioning to demonstrate how changes in the material construction of buildings and houses, backed by public policies and regulations, has been highly successful in the transformation to high energy cooling habits in the USA and Japan, and more recently in India, Southeast Asian countries and China, where the use of air conditioning is expected to exceed the USA by 2020. According to a recent study by the Netherlands Environmental Assessment Agency, air conditioning could contribute 25 percent of global carbon emissions by 2025. (NEAA 2015). Until the mid-twentieth century, in the warmer regions in the USA and elsewhere, houses were designed to accommodate the heat through ventilation-friendly designs and materials. Ventilation and air flow was augmented in the twentieth century with electric fans, which use very little energy. From the mid-twentieth century, first in the USA and later spreading to Japan and other countries in Asia, Africa and Latin America, buildings began to be designed to be cooled with a combination of air conditioners and tight structures to keep the mechanically cooled air from leaking out. Cooper (1998) shows how this regime change in cooling comfort in the USA was promoted by a coordinated effort of powerful economic actors including the energy industry, the construction industry, the manufacturing industry and the banking industry, all of whom reaped huge economic benefits from air-conditioned comfort. According to the US Department of Energy (2009), in 2009 two thirds of all homes in the United States had air conditioners, consuming about 5 percent of all the electricity produced in the United States, and emitting 100 million tons of CO_2 each year – an average of about two tonnes of CO_2 for each home with an air conditioner. In Chapter 2 I related how these same actors, both transnational and local, contributed to the air conditioning of Japan from the 1960s to the 1990s. In 2010, 80 percent of all homes in Japan were air conditioned. The use of air conditioning is also growing in Europe. The European Union predicts that over the next 15 years, the energy used to cool European buildings is likely to rise by 72 percent (EU 2015).

My research in Kerala (Wilhite 2008) revealed how the changes in the way houses are built are forcing changes in cooling and other home habits in India. The use of wood, plaster (laterite) and clay in building construction, all of which facilitate draughts, are being replaced by less costly, concrete constructions, both in public buildings and in house construction. Concrete is the construction material of choice for new houses, both for walls and roofs, replacing thatch (coconut leaves and straw) or clay tiles that allow the air to flow and the heat to escape. Concrete is cheap and durable, but concrete structures are very difficult to keep cool without the air conditioners. The building construction industry is driving growth in the cement industry of about 10 percent per year, one of the fastest growing industries in India. In addition to using mainly coal-based fossil fuels in concrete production, CO_2 is emitted in the chemical processes used to produce concrete. The high price of air conditioners made them prohibitive for most middle-class Indian families until the 1990s. There were only a few Indian air conditioning manufacturers prior to the economic liberalization in 1991 and a lack of competition contributed to high prices. Prices for air conditioners fell rapidly in the 1990s, when the excise tax was eliminated and import restrictions on air conditioners relaxed. In 2001, air conditioners were removed from the luxury goods category and the 18.75 percent luxury tax dropped. By 2002 there were more than 17 major air conditioning brands on the Indian market, most of them foreign (some with licensed production in India) offering about 60 different air-conditioning models. By 2005, air-conditioning sales in India were growing at 20 percent per year. As Indian families adjust to air-conditioned living, new practices develop that lock out the outside environment and lock in the cooled air. Doors and windows remain closed, and life moves from gardens and front porches to enclosed living rooms. In 2015, air conditioning was responsible for 40 percent of the electricity demand in Mumbai. It is estimated that 60 percent of Indian houses will be air conditioned by 2030 (Guardian 2015).

Hansen et al. (2016) relate how a similar transformation is taking place in post-*Doi Moi* economic liberalization in communist Vietnam. *Doi Moi* was a series of economic reforms initiated in 1986 and opened for the market economy and private enterprises, as well as introducing land reforms and the decollectivization of agriculture. *Doi Moi* also brought a rapid increase in the availability of goods and a growing middle class with the purchasing power to acquire them. Vietnam had one of the fastest growing economies in the world over the two last decades, growing at about the same rate as India at 7 percent annually. As late as in 2002, there was on average one air conditioner per 100 households. This increased to 11.5 per cent in 2012. According to Hansen et al., a decade later in 2012, one third of urban households owned an air conditioner and the market for air conditioners is expected to grow at a rate of close to 8 per cent annually in the coming years. In 2012, 97 percent of hotels and 58 percent of offices in Vietnam were air conditioned. Rimmer and Dick (2009) surveyed air conditioning across South Asia and found a similar growth in air conditioning in virtually all South East Asian cities. Sahakian (2014) finds the same rapid spread of air conditioning to buildings and houses in major cities in the Philippines.

In the USA and Europe, this mechanically produced comfort regime was extended decades ago into automobiles, trains, buses and metro systems. Parkhurst and Parnaby (2008) found that the percentage of cars with built-in air conditioners increased in Europe from 20 to 70 percent within a few years in the late 1990s, and by 2015 was approaching 90 percent. In an article entitled 'conditioning of comfort', I suggested that the air conditioning of spaces for home, work, shopping and transportation produced bodies that cannot tolerate doing any of these activities in natural settings (Wilhite 2009). Wallenborn and Wilhite (2014: 61) express this bodily transformation thus: 'The transition from lives that involve movement between contrasting climatic spaces, to lives in thermally homogeneous spaces leads to a reconfiguration of the body and its sensations, and even a kind of oblivion of the body'. Life in a building designed for natural cooling involves an active interaction between occupant and building in order to regulate shading and draughts. The mechanization of comfort, promoted by governments, commercial actors and lending institutions, has limited flexibility and made cooling comfort energy dependent. As Murphey (2006: 151) writes, in the home, car and workplace, 'The inside, brought about by the built environments of late capitalism, provides your habitat, the milieu for your embodiment'. Habits formed in conditioned spaces designed and built for 22°C year round will be very difficult to break and reform. A conservative prediction is that unless the conditions for home cooling and refrigeration are reshaped, refrigerated comfort will be the source of 30 percent of all climate emissions in 2030 (Munzinger and Gessner 2015).

This delegation of comfort to buildings and technologies is having a backlash in many urban areas around the world. Commercial buildings made of concrete, glass and steel quickly gain heat, making air conditioning necessary to create conditions comfortable enough to work in hot climates. In several parts of the world where electricity delivery systems are strained, such as in Japanese and Australian cities, the inability to supply enough electricity to meet peak loads in the warmest part of the day has led to changes in the way people dress and move. In Japan, the government has issued guidelines intended to eliminate the wearing of business suits and ties at workplaces so that thermostat settings can be raised during peak summer heat. The electricity utilities have introduced tariffs in which companies agree to shut off air conditioners during the hottest periods of the day in return for a rebate or reduction in electricity tariffs. In 2005, the government passed new regulations for government buildings that mandated a minimum setting of air-conditioning thermostats at 28 degrees and combined this with a dress policy disallowing the wearing of ties in the workplace. The new clothing practice, more amenable to warmer temperatures, allowed for less energy-driven cooling and an estimated annual reduction in CO_2 emissions of 1.14 million tonnes, as well as a reduction in the sale of ties by 36 percent (Ehrhardt-Martinez et al. 2015). Japanese and Australians, living and working among the most advanced and richest countries of the world, find themselves in the ironic situation that they must develop new ways to stay comfortable when they have to turn up air-conditioning thermostats in buildings with very tight thermal envelopes. An important point is that these changes were adaptive rather than proactive. The limits of what the electricity system could deliver forced changes in comfort and clothing practices. Should we continue to emit carbon beyond the levels of what the ecosystem can tolerate, the adaptations will force significant changes in everyday practices of people everywhere that are much more severe than the adjustments in clothing and cooling practices in Japan, especially in the vulnerable coastal regions and climate-sensitive food-producing regions of the world. Deep changes will have to be proactive and start now. In the domain of the house, this means retaining and reinforcing the design, materials and practices of non-mechanical cooling and an intensified effort to design modern buildings that can tolerate warm climates with little or no mechanical cooling.

Clean and presentable bodies

The commodification of what it means to be clean and beautiful has been a work in progress over the past century in Europe, the USA and other rich countries of the world, the consequence of which has been an emergence of habits that demand high amounts of energy and water. Over the past few decades, these Western cleaning and beauty practices have expanded globally through globalizing markets and media. Historian Katherine Ashenburg (2007) has researched bathing practices over time and cross-culturally. She writes that in the twentieth century, the definition of cleanliness was 'a work in progress' in which commercial interests played a key role in constantly redefining the meaning of what it is to be clean. Bodily cleanliness became one of the most effective subjects for commercial advertising. Various forms of smells were discursively invented and identified as evidence of poor body hygiene. One of the early examples of this was the company Listerine's christening of a malady they labelled 'halitosis' – chronic bad breath – in the 1920s. Listerine could then claim in a very successful marketing strategy that their toothpaste and mouthwash would cure halitosis. Other commercial marketing strategies by corporate soap manufacturers have created the maladies of 'problem perspiration' and 'body odour', both of which could be covered or eliminated by perfume and perfumed soap and deodorant.

By the early twentieth century, cleaning and beauty products were popular enough to justify the creation of a specific retail outlet to display and sell them – the pharmacy, or drug store. Ivan Illich (1976), quoted in Ashenburg (2007: 243), writes that 'Ultimately the drugstore became the symbol of the industrialized aura; it is the supermarket of mass-produced glamour and scents for a deodorized population. People who obsessively scrub away their auras can pick and choose a better one there.' The drug store faded out of the retail landscape in the 1970s, or more accurately, faded into larger retail megastores such as Walgreens and Walmart. Nonetheless, the sections in these and other major retail corporations devoted to body care continued to grow over the course of the century in terms of products offered and space dedicated to their display and sale. Smith (2007: 329) writes that 'Well-packaged cleansing products such as liquid detergents, spray polish, bathroom cleaners, air fresheners, liquid soaps, and shower gels began to fill the post-war house with perfume – a stunning array'. An expanding beauty regime consisting of soaps (face, hands and body), shampoo, hair conditioner, perfume, skin-cleaning products and coloured cosmetics has contributed to a billion-dollar industry and a globalizing international beauty norm. Recent additions to the internationalizing beauty norm include hair treatments, frequent pedicures and manicures, depilation, skin waxing and moisturizing. Until mid-twentieth century, the bulk of these products were made for women, but both Ashenburg and Virginia Smith (2007) relate how the beauty industry has extended its market to include men. According to a 2014 market survey discussed by Smith, male perfume products make up one third of perfume sales in the USA. Clean smells have also been incorporated into products designed to clean the house and clothes. According to Moran et al. (2012), the cleaning product industry is now a multibillion-dollar global industry.

Body beauty and cleanliness are attended to mainly in the bathroom, the number and size of which have increased over the past half century. In Europe the bathroom did not enter the four walls of the house until the mid-twentieth century. As late as 1954, only one in ten Frenchmen had a bathroom in their house (Ashenburg 2007: 274). From the 1960s, the number and size of bathrooms have increased in all European countries. A study by Hand, Shove and Southerton (2007) found that the construction of multiple bathrooms was a major reason for home extensions in Great Britain in the late 1990s. They relate this to an increase in the availability of home loans for renovation, as well as a desire to increase the value of the house. Another widely shared motive was to alleviate the 'rush' for the bathroom in the morning as householders get ready for work. In houses with more than one person living in them, a second bathroom reduces waiting for the regular morning shower, applying cosmetic products and making other bodily preparations.

In the USA in 1929, the average home had one bathroom. In the 1950s, houses began to be built with a second bathroom or toilet. In 2005, 24 percent of all newly constructed houses had three or more bathrooms and by 2010 the average house had 2.5 bathrooms. Ashenburg found that in houses built for rich and upper middle-class households in the USA it is becoming more common to build master bedrooms with two bathrooms, one for each of the occupants. She also found that the size of bathrooms in the USA is increasing, tripling in size in the decade between 1994 and 2004. The frequency of bathing is also increasing in both the USA and Europe. Ashenburg writes that 'In North America today, there seems to be no resting place, no point at which we can feel comfortable in our own skins for more than a few hours after our last shower. "Clean" keeps receding into the distance' (2007: 271). Shove (2003) relates how in the course of one generation in Europe, bodily cleaning was transformed from weekly bathing to near daily showering. Shower gels, shampoos and hair conditioning treatments have become normal adjuncts to the shower, the use of which extends the length of the shower and the amount of water used. Shove writes that longer showers contributed to a dramatic increase of 70 percent in domestic water consumption in the UK between 1970 and 2000. Taken together, cleaning in the form of bathing, showering and washing clothes is responsible for about a third of water consumption in the UK.

The frequency of clothes washing is increasing in all of the OECD countries. In a study of clothes-washing habits in Melbourne, Australia reported by Jack (2013), respondents in the study were asked how often they washed their jeans and what was important to their decision on when to wash. Only 31 percent used 'visible dirt' as the prompt to wash the jeans. Over 60 percent reported that they 'always' washed their jeans after 2–3 wearings and over 50 percent attributed this to 'habit'. In a study of clothes-laundering practices in the UK, Mylan (2015) cites a DEFRA (2012) study that found that UK households do on average 285 laundry loads per year. Based on interviews with households, Mylan found that 'items of clothing are laundered not only to remove dirt, but for a whole host of purposes such as to remove odour, to disinfect and to "freshen up"' (2015: 17).

Efforts in the UK to reduce the energy needed to support clothes-washing habits has been indifferent to the number of washings and has rather focused on reducing the temperature of the water at which laundry is washed, a policy pattern of turning a blind eye to volume that we see in virtually every policy domain concerned with reducing energy and carbon. According to Mylan, the overall frequency of washing has increased, not because of concerns with hygiene but because of the association of clean clothes with good smells, softness and brightness. She writes that the reduction in washing temperature has provided a lucrative market for soap manufacturers who produce and sell a new range of soaps that are claimed to be more effective at low temperatures, as well as new products for pre-treatments and additives, while maintaining markets for standard detergents used in higher-temperature washing of items such as towels, bedsheets and diapers. These studies in Australia and the UK are consistent with the findings of Pierce et al. (2010) from the USA: cleanliness is no longer only about removing dirt and good hygiene, but about producing good smells and achieving a soft and shiny appearance. Energy savings targets associated with public policy that aims at increased washing efficiency (water and energy) are being overwhelmed by increases in volume of bathrooms, showers, clothes washing and associated com- modities, all of which use energy and emit carbon and other pollutants. In a growing and geographically expanding capitalist economy this combination of growth, commodification and individualization will inevitably outstrip increased efficiency in the demands of energy, water and pollutants in household comfort and body habits. I will address this problem of this 'rebound effect' in Chapter 4.

The global capitalist reach of transnational corporations and media is extending these Western comfort, beauty and cleaning norms to Asia and Africa (Wilhite 2008 and 2014; Comaroff and Comaroff 1992; Burke 2003). In India, the post-1991 wave of transnational corporate investment, supported by inter- national development agencies such as the International Monetary Fund, World Bank and regional development banks, introduced new soap products in India. Many of the marketing discourses for selling soap in nineteenth- and twentieth- century North America have been used in Indian advertising. Perfumed soaps have been heavily marketed. The 'fragrance' market, consisting of perfumes, perfumed soaps and body creams, grew at 15 percent per year in India in the early 2000s (Phookan 2004). Body odour and 'germs' have been advertised as targets for soap. The World Bank has initiated and funded 'hand-washing' campaigns in several Indian states, using soap products produced by the transnational soap corpora- tions Palmolive and Lever Brothers. These have created markets for soap and in some parts of India with low rainfall (and limited water for hand washing) may have positive effects on hygiene, but in states with high rainfall such as Kerala, good hygiene has been achieved without the use of excessive soap. The increase in the use of soap is an unneeded expense for low-income households, and the grey run-off from excess soap is polluting water sources (Wilhite 2008).

The consumption of beauty products such as lipstick, nail polish, eye liner and other cosmetics are also growing rapidly in India, with the vast majority of products sold produced by beauty transnationals such as Unilever, Colgate Palmolive and Procter and Gamble (Hansen et al. 2016). Many of these pro- ducts capitalize on the Indian, and pan-Asian, interest in fair skin and in the use of powders, creams and treatments to lighten skin. After the 1991 economic liber- alization, transnational soap and cosmetic corporations developed and created markets for a new range of fairness-oriented powders, creams and oils. Both Indian and foreign-based fairness products are some of the most heavily advertised on Indian television. Beauty salons offer 'fairness treatments' based on chemical bleaching of the skin, most of the clients being women of marriageable age, when young women come under intense scrutiny by the families of prospective grooms. A recent market survey in India shows that the use of fairness products is also growing among men. Monica Chada (2005) cites market surveys that indicate that 29 percent of Indian men were using fairness products in 2005. Hansen et al. (Hansen et al. 2016) write that India's whitening cream market reportedly grew from USD 397 million in 2008 to USD 638 million in 2012. Goon and Craven (2003) demonstrate that the fairness market is a pan-Asian market, with the purchase of fairness products growing in China, Vietnam, Malaysia and Indonesia. Globally, beauty and cleanliness habits are expanding in step with expanding capitalism to include the application and use of an increasing number of commodities to keep pace with changing beauty norms.

Women are the main targets of marketing strategies for promoting household cleaning appliances in North America, Europe and more recently in India, China and Vietnam. The marketing claim is that washing machines, tumble dryers and dishwashers will make the housewife who uses them capable and efficient (Cowan 1983). An advertising brochure produced by the electricity industry in 1920s England demonstrates an early example of this global marketing discourse: 'With the help of Electricity you can do the housework without making more work and clean the Home without making yourself dirty...ELECTRICITY is the cleanest, hardest working, most willing and cheapest servant under the sun. Always on duty, ready for instant service, day and night at the touch of a switch' (cited in Smith 2007: 314). Appliances such as the vacuum cleaner, washing machine, dishwasher and tumble dryer would save time and physical work. They would make time management possible for the 'working housewife' who, with the help of household appliances, could accomplish both salaried work and house-work, and for those not working outside the home, provide time for leisure and self-improvement.

The contention that household cleaning appliances have actually saved women time is controversial and the subject of academic debate contributed to by both sociologists of consumption and feminist scholars. In her book *More Work for Mother*, Cowan (1983) argued that domestic appliances simply fragmented time and produced a greater number of domestic tasks. Hochschild (1997) argued that these technologies turned the home into a 'second shift' which has ended up with the vicious cycle described by Schor (1993) in which households need to work more in order to consume more. In my research in India, I observed that the time-saving potential of household appliances was heavily marketed and that saving time for working women was one of the central motives for purchasing washing machines, food processing devices and refrigerators. However, consistent with the findings of Cowen, the ownership of these appliances did not alter gender roles and responsibilities in the execution of household and family chores or reduce the time used by women on house and family care (Wilhite 2008).

Transport

Thousands of pages have been written about the importance of the automobile to capitalist expansion. Featherstone captures this in his quote from 2004: 'The visibility and influence of the car as a key object of mass production (Fordism) and mass consumption, the impact on spatial organization through roads, city layout, suburban housing and shopping malls, are undisputed. There is a powerful socio-economic and technological complex at work sustaining the car' (2004: 1). In other words, if there is any single commodity that can be said to be the icon of modernity and development in both household consumption and in national economy it is the car. The bundle of infrastructures and technologies premiering the car has locked transport in the USA and parts of Europe into automobility. As Urry (2004: 28) writes, 'automobility has extended individual freedom and flexibility, but has also constrained "car users" to live their lives in spatially stretched and time-compressed ways. The car is the literal "iron cage" of modernity, motorized, moving and domestic.'

The growth of the automobile and the habits of automobility are related to the growth in production and consumption of a myriad of other commodities associated with the car, including the petroleum products needed to propel it. Automobility has been the object of massive public investment in road infra-structure in the form of intercity highways and urban roads. Urry summarizes the car's inroads into various facets of industrial development as follows: the car is implicated in 'An extraordinarily powerful *complex* constituted through technical and social interlinkages with other industries, car parts and acces-sories; petrol refining and distribution; road-building and maintenance; hotels, roadside service areas and motels; car sales and repair workshops; suburban house building; retailing and leisure complexes; advertising and marketing; urban design and planning' (2004: 26)

The cities of the 20th and 21st centuries have been and continue to be designed and built for the car. These urban structures are literally set in concrete and will require massive investment if they are to be remade in ways that facilitate other forms of transportation. Thus it can be said that the elements discussed in Chapter 2 that enable habit formation are in place when it comes to the car: material infrastructures built to support the car, public and media discourses associating the car with the good life, and several generations of experience in the USA and Europe immersed in car culture. As Edensor writes, 'The road and roadside form a largely unquestioned backdrop to driving routines, tasks, pleasures and movements in which we unreflexively carry out quotidian manoeuvres and modes of dwelling as habituated body subjects' (2004: 109).

The individualizing forces of capitalism are evident in shaping the ownership and uses of the car. Until the mid-century, the car was mainly associated with family. Car manufacturers marketed the 'family car' as an essential adjunct to home and household tasks. There should be 'a car in every garage', as Herbert Hoover repeated time and again in his presidential campaign of 1928. The car in mid-century USA was marketed as a shared family possession, the use of which was to be coordinated by the adults in the family and used for vacations and 'Sunday drives' by the entire family. From the 1970s the 'two-car family' replaced the 'family car' in marketing and the 'two-car garage' became standard for middle-class suburban homes. A car for each of the adults would allow the family greater independence in multiple tasks such as commuting to individual jobs; shopping; transporting children to kindergartens and schools; and driving to hobbies, beauty parlours and training studios. As Featherstone writes (2004: 12),

> with the increase in the numbers of working women, the separation of home from work, the need for mothers to transport children to school and friends and the key role women have in organizing household consumption, the car has become essential in juggling the everyday time economy. For many women the car is central to the logistics of maintaining mundane everyday household relationships. At the same time it can also be the avenue of escape or inversion of this routine multi-tasking.

This individualizing of the car has contributed to a multiplication of the number of cars bought and used in everyday life, thus increasing the need for road space, parking and intercity highway lanes. The car has affected urban design and engendered a new form of retail shopping, the 'shopping centre' or 'shopping mall', a concentration of retail stores, often under a single roof (mechanically heated and cooled) and surrounded by giant parking lots. Shopping centres multiplied in the late twentieth century, situated mainly on the peripheries of cities where large tracts of land were available. The resulting car-designed urban environment has 'unbundled territorialities of home, work, business and leisure that historically were closely integrated, and fragmented social practices in shared public spaces' (Urry 2004: 28). This new urban landscape put many local, neighbourhood and city-centre shops out of business, disabling the shopping practice of walking or cycling to nearby shops. The combination of the car and the household refrigerator/freezer allows for buying 'in bulk' and is contributing to significant changes in food habits.

One billion cars were manufactured in the twentieth century (Urry 2004). Automobility expanded over the course of the century measured in terms of cars owned, number of cars per household, number of kilometres driven and size of individual cars. In the USA by 2009 there were on average 2.28 vehicles per household. Over 31 percent of households owned two cars and 35 percent own three cars or more (http://press.experian.com/United-States/Press-Release/new-study-shows-multiple-cars-are-king-in-american-households.aspx). According to the US Department of Transportation Federal Highway Administration, the average American driver drove 13,476 miles (21,561 km) in 2010, or 60 km per day. The increase in miles travelled from 1990 to 2014 compensated for gains in fuel efficiency in the USA so that the total amount of annual fuel consumption remained at about the same level over the period. Car mobility is increasing rapidly in the 'emerging economies' of China, India, Vietnam and Brazil. In China, the number of cars and drivers has now exceeded that of the USA. There are 35 Chinese cities with more than 1 million automobiles. As Whitelegg (1997), cited in Urry (2004: 25) writes, the car is the 'predominant global form of "quasi-private" *mobility* that subordinates other mobilities of walking, cycling, travelling by rail and so on, and reorganizes how people negotiate the opportunities for, and constraints upon, work, family life, child-hood, leisure and pleasure'. The car has made a deep imprint on travel habits, urban design and visions of progress and development. In Chapter 5 I will take up the question of how to break the car's hold on transport habits and enable alternative modes of transport.

Refrigeration and refrigerator-dependent food habits

The refrigerator shares with the automobile the qualities of allowing for speed (reduced shopping, quick preparation of meals), but in contrast to the auto-mobile is a technology placed 'inconspicuously' in kitchens and garages (Shove and Warde 2002). It has been identified as a 'white good' that performs its task of producing chilled air with virtually no need for intervention or management by the owner. In fact Shove and Southerton (2000), drawing on the work of Forty (1986), suggest that the functional styling and white appearance of refrigerators and freezers was intended by manufacturers to associate these appliances with other practical household appliances such as the stove, washing machine, tumble dryer and dishwasher that promised to make household tasks more efficient, orderly and hygienic. By the twenty-first century in Europe and the USA, the refrigerator/freezer has come to be regarded as an indispensable appliance and a taken-for-granted component in everyday food practices. Its size and functions have expanded in step with growth in the economy, the house and the things in it.

Prior to the advent of the refrigerator, food was kept cool in basements, darkened closets and, in rural settings in the USA, 'cellars' dug into backyards. These food-storage practices took advantage of natural cooling provided by shading and ventilation, but they did not provide sufficiently cool temperatures to sustain the quality of most varieties of food for more than a day or two. The 'ice box', invented in the 1800s in England, was intended to provide cooler temperatures, allowing for longer storage of foods. It consisted of two cabinets, one for food and the other, lined with zinc or tin, for the ice to cool the food cabinet. My great grandmother, who lived in rural Texas, bought an ice box around 1910 that is still in my possession. The cabinet for storing food is only about 0.10 cubic meters, enough space for a bottle of milk, a few eggs and fresh vegetables. By contrast, the average refrigerator cabinet in the USA today is over four times that size, 0.45 cubic meters (Fay 2015).

The first mechanically cooled refrigerator was produced in 1913 and the Frigidaire Company began mass producing refrigerators for the US market in 1918. By 1929, 1 million refrigerators had been produced and sold in the USA. The refrigerator's colder storage temperatures were achieved through a combination of electricity, a compressor, coolants and insulation. This extended the life of fresh products such as vegetables, meats and dairy products, and made possible the growth of entirely new food regimes, such as bottled drinks. The later addition of a small freezer to the same appliance allowed for the storage of frozen foods and ready-made frozen meals. As with the car, an extensive infrastructure and system of provision grew up around the refrigerator, including refrigerated warehouses for wholesale storage, refrigerated transport to bring foods to retail stores, and refrigerated sections of the retail food stores where the products are displayed and sold. The combination of the refrigerator and the car transformed shopping habits in many parts of the world from frequent shopping in local markets or small retail stores to less frequent shopping for larger amounts of food in supermarkets. Over the course of three generations in Europe and the USA, the refrigerator has transformed eating and food shopping habits. Its role has changed from that of accessory to food preparation to being absolutely essential, both because it saves time (shopping time and food preparation time) and because of changing food practices that are increasingly centred on ready-made and frozen foods.

Shove and Southerton (2000) relate how the freezer has become an indispensable node in food production and consumption in the United Kingdom over the course of a 30-year period. In 1965, only 3 percent of UK households owned a freezer. By 1995, ownership had increased to 97 percent. They attribute this rapid diffusion to time pressures related to women entering the workforce in great numbers from the 1970s. As in the marketing discourses associated with cleaning appliances discussed above, the freezer is marketed to the efficient housewife as a 'time machine' (in the words of Shove and Southerton) that helps women accomplish all of the tasks that make up time-stressed days. The freezer was conjoined with the refrigerator in the 1980s and provided a 'mini-supermarket' within the home containing 'freezer-dependent foods such as burgers, pizzas and iced cream' (Shove and Southerton 2000: 308). The refrigerator/freezer has become so embedded in the fabric of food preparation in the USA and Europe that specialty stores and large sections of supermarkets are dedicated to frozen foods and convenience foods. 'The freezers of today promise to help people cope with the compression and fragmentation of time. But in so doing they lock their users into certain practices and habits, at the same time requiring an extensive if routinely invisible supporting infrastructure' (Shove and Southerton 2000: 315).

Refrigeration and freezing have also been essential to the growth in meat and dairy consumption over the past half century. A study of meat consumption in the USA by Larsen (2012) showed that as refrigerators became standard home appliances in the 1950s, meat consumption began to increase. From 1950 to 2010 annual meat consumption increased by five times in the USA to an estimated 50 billion pounds of meat, corresponding to an annual beef consumption of 42 kg per person. The consequences for land use and the consumption of energy and water have been dramatic. Kapper (2014) estimates that to prepare one 'quarter pound' hamburger requires 6.7 pounds of grain and forage for the cattle, 52.8 gallons of water, 74.5 square feet of land and 1,000 BTUs of energy. Beef grazing, livestock production and meat distribution account for about 50 percent of climate emissions in the USA. In the UK, Oosterveer and Sonnenfeld (2012) estimate that meat and dairy consumption contribute 66 percent of carbon emissions from food-related activities. The global climate emissions attributable to meat production and consumption are 25 times that of rice (Weber and Matthews 2008).

In addition to enabling energy-intensive food practices, the electricity needed to run refrigerators is significant. In the European Union, about 15 percent of household energy use goes to cold appliances (refrigerators and freezers) and in European supermarkets, refrigeration accounts for up to 50 percent of the building's energy consumption. The energy efficiency of the refrigerator compressor has increased over the past three decades, but the total amount of the electricity used by refrigerators has only declined slightly over the same period because of the increase in the size and number of refrigerators per household (McNary and Berry 2012). In 2008, 99 percent of homes in the United States had one refrigerator and about 26 percent had two or more (34 percent of California homes had two or more refrigerators) (US Department of Energy 2009). In the UK, where only about one in three houses had a refrigerator in 1960, today over 95 percent of households own one.

Refrigerator-dependent energy and carbon-intensive food practices are diffusing globally. In China, household refrigerator ownership rose from 7 percent in 1995 to 95 percent in 2007. My research in India revealed that refrigeration is a powerful change agent that affects both eating and food shopping habits (Wilhite 2008). Most South Indians were initially only mildly interested in the refrigerator when it was introduced into India in the 1960s, mainly due to a longstanding food ideology that associates the storing of prepared foods with the accumulation of substances which cause laziness and stupidity. Food should be 'alive' in order to give life to the eater. Eating foods that had been refrigerated and reheated was thought to be associated with digestion problems and lethargy. Another related belief was that cold foods and drinks, including chilled water, cause sore throats, colds and stomach problems. My research revealed that as women enter the workforce yet retain responsibility for food preparation and other household chores, refrigerators were being purchased in order to save shopping and preparation time. Many young women now routinely make food in bulk, store uneaten portions and reheat them for later meals. As refrigerators are taken into use and become routine aspects of food preparation, ideologies relating stored food to laziness and bad health are dissolving.

Conclusion

The examples in this chapter reveal how high energy habits have emerged in step with the emergence of capitalist political economy in the USA and Europe, and are spreading to other parts of the world through transnational capitalism and increasing global trade. The energy and carbon intensity of the ways people practice thermal comfort, cleanliness, transport and food are anchored in political economies premiering growth, commodification and individualization and in some high energy domains such as home comfort, cleaning and transport are locked into material landscapes and infrastructures that will have to be unlocked and refashioned if deep reductions in energy use and carbon emissions are to be possible. The social, cultural and material filaments connecting capitalist political economy to high energy habits inhibit the capacity to reduce energy demand

and carbon emissions related to comfort, food and travel. Reforming habits will be a prodigious enterprise, but the historical examples given in this chapter show that change is possible and that twentieth-century changes from expansive to contractive consumption in the mid-twentieth century and back again after World War II were related to expansive and contractive periods in global and national economies. The post-World War II economic expansion has been intentional, limitless and associated with increased human development and wellbeing. The challenge from a low carbon perspective will be to intentionally contract the economies of the rich countries of the world, their household habits and their carbon emissions in ways that maintain high life quality, while allowing developing countries to expand their economies. In the next chapter I review and assess the weaknesses of mainstream low carbon theories, which are predicated on the fallacy that deep reductions in carbon are possible in capitalist, growth-oriented economies.

References

Appadurai, A. 1996. *Modernity at Large: Cultural Dimensions of Globalization.* Minneapolis and London: University of Minnesota Press.

Ashenburg, Katherine. 2007. *The Dirt on Clean: An Unsanitized History.* New York: North Point Press.

Bourdieu, P. 1984. *Distinction: A Social Critique of the Judgement of Taste.* London: Routledge and Kegan Paul.

Burke, T. 2003. *Lifebuoy Men, Lux Women: Commodification, Consumption and Cleanliness in Modern Zimbabwe.* Durham, NC and London: Duke University Press.

Chada, Monica. 2005Indian Men Go Tall, Fair and Handsome *BBC News.* Available at http://news.bbc.co.uk/2/hi/south_asia/4396122.stm. Accessed 1 December 2015.

Cohen, Lizabeth. 2003. *A Consumer's Republic: The Politics of Mass Consumption in Postwar America.* New York: Knopf.

Comaroff, John and Jean Comaroff. 1992. *Ethnography and Historical Imagination.* Boulder, CO: Westview Press.

Cooper, Gail. 1998. *Air Conditioning America: Engineers and the Controlled Environment, 1900–1960.* Baltimore, MD: Johns Hopkins University Press.

Cowan, Ruth Schwartz. 1983. *More Work for Mother: The Ironies of Household Technology from the Open Hearth to the Microwave.* New York: Basic Books.

Cross, Gary. 2000. *An All-Consuming Century: Why Commercialism Won in Modern America.* New York: Colombia University Press.

CSE. 2015. Assessing US Climate Action Plan. Report by the Centre for Science and Environment, Delhi. Available at http://www.cse.org. Accessed 17 October 2015.

DEFRA. 2012. *Household Electricity Study EV0702: Final Report.* London: Department of the Environment, Food and Rural Affairs.

Edensor, T. 2004. Automobility and National Identity: Representation, Geography and Driving Practice. *Theory, Culture and Society* 21(4/5): 101–120.

Ehrhardt-Martinez, Karen, Juliet B. Schor, Wokje Abrahamse, Alison Alkon, Jon Axsen, Keith Brown, Rachel Shwom, Dale Southerton and Harold Wilhite. 2015. Consumption and Climate Change. In Riley E. Dunlap and Robert J. Brulle (eds), *Climate Change and Society: Sociological Perspectives.* Oxford: Oxford University Press.

Energy Savings Trust. 2009. *Powering the Nation: Household Electricity-Using Habits Revealed*. London: Energy Savings Trust.

Energy Savings Trust. 2014. *The Elephant in the Living Room: How Our Appliances and Gadgets Are Trampling the Green Dream*. London: Energy Savings Trust.

EU. 2015. Cleaner Cooling: Sustainably Meeting the Rapid Growth in Transport and Urban Cooling Demand. Available at http://www.eusew.eu/component/see_eventview/?view=see_eventdetail&mapType=hlpc&eventid=5394. Accessed 27 October 2015.

Fay, K. L. 2015. Dimensions of a Standard Sized Refrigerator. Published by SFGate. Available at http://homeguides.sfgate.com/dimensions-standard-size-refrigerator-82262.html. Accessed 1 October 2015.

Featherstone, Mike. 2004. Automobilities: An Introduction. *International Journal of Urban and Regional Research* 24(4): 1–24.

Forty, A. 1986. *Objects of Desire: Design and Society since 1750*. London: Thames and Hudson.

Fox, Frank W. 1975. *Madison Avenue Goes to War: The Strange Military career of American Advertising, 1941–45*. Provo, UT: Brigham Young University Press.

Goon, P. and A. Craven. 2003. Whose Debt? Globalization and White Facing in Asia. *Intersections: Gender, History and Culture in the Asian Context* 9. Available at http://intersections.anu.edu.au/issue9/gooncraven.html. Accessed 9 July 2015.

Guardian. 2015. India's Rising Demands for Cooling Make It a Hot Topic. Available at http://www.theguardian.com/world/2015/oct/26/india-rising-demands-cooling-hot-topic. Accessed 27 October 2015.

Gunderson, Dana. 2013. Your Scraps Add Up. New York: National Resources Defense Council, March. Available at http://www.nrdc.org/living/eatingwell/files/foodwaste_2pgr.pdf. Accessed 27 September 2015.

Hand, Martin, Elizabeth Shove and Dale Southerton. 2007. Home Extensions in the United Kingdom: Space, Time, and Practice. *Environment and Planning D: Society and Space* 25: 668–681.

Hansen, Arve, Harold Wilhite and Kenneth Nielsen. 2016. Staying Cool, Looking Good, Moving Around: Consumption, Sustainability and the 'Rise of the South'. *Forum for Development Studies*. Available at: http://dx.doi.org/10.1080/08039410.2015.1134640.

Hanssen, Ole Jørgen and Hanne Møller. 2013. Matsvinn i Norge 2013: Status og utviklingstrekk 2009–2013. Østlandsforsking Report OR.32.13, Norway.

Haugen, Yngvild Pernell. 2008. The Norwegian Cabin Life in Transition: Implications for the Consumption of Energy. Masters thesis, Centre for Development and the Environment, University of Oslo.

Hochschild, Arlie Russell. 1997. *The Time Bind: When Work Becomes Time and Time Becomes Work*. New York: Henry Holt and Company.

Illich, Ivan. 1976. *Medical Nemesis: The Expropriation of Health*. New York: Pantheon Books.

Jack, Tullia. 2013. Nobody Was Dirty: Intervening in Inconspicuous Consumption of Laundry Routines. *Journal of Consumer Culture*, published online, doi: 10.1177/1469540513485272.

Jones, Christopher and Daniel Kammen. 2011. Quantifying Carbon Footprint Reduction Opportunities for US Households and Communities. *Environmental Science and Technology* 45(9): 4088–4095.

Kapper, Jude L. 2014. US Beef Industry's Environmental Impact. WWF webinar, September. Available at https://www.academia.edu/8201264/The_U.S._Beef_Industry_s_Environmental_Impact. Accessed 4 September 2015.

Larsen, Janet. 2012. Peak Meat: U.S. Meat Consumption Falling. Data Highlights. New Brunswick, NJ: Earth Policy Institute. Available at http://www.earth-policy.org/data_highlights/2012/highlights25. Accessed 8 July 2015.

McNary, Bill and Chip Berry. 2012. *How Americans Are Using Energy in Homes Today.* Proceedings of the 2012 ACEEE Summer Study in Buildings. Washington, DC: American Council for an Energy Efficient Economy.

Moran, Rebecca E., Deborah H. Bennett, Daniel J. Tancredi, Xiangmei Wu, Beate Ritz and Irva Hertz-Picciotto. 2012. Frequency and Longitudinal Trends of Household Care Product Use. *Atmospheric Environment* 55: 417–424.

Munzinger, Philipp and Alexandra Gessner. 2015. Climate-Friendly Refrigeration and Air Conditioning: A Key Mitigation Option for INDCs. Working paper, *GIZ*, September. Available at http://www.giz.de/expertise/downloads/giz2015-en-rac-sector-indcs.pdf. Accessed 6 April 2015.

Murphey, Michelle. 2006. *Sick Building Syndrome and the Problem of Uncertainty: Environmental Politics, Technoscience and Women Workers.* Durham, NC and London: Duke University Press.

Mylan, Josephine. 2015. Understanding the Diffusion of Sustainable Product-Service Systems: Insights from the Sociology of Consumption and Practice Theory. *Journal of Cleaner Production* 97: 13–20.

NEAA. 2015. Co-Benefits of Climate Policy. Report by the Netherlands Environmental Assessment Agency. Available at http://www.unep.org/transport/gfei/autotool/understanding_the_problem/Netherlands%20Environment%20Agency.pdf. Accessed 27 October 2015.

Oosterveer, Peter and David A. Sonnenfeld. 2012. *Food, Globalization and Sustainability.* London and New York: Earthscan.

Parkhurst, G. and R. Parnaby. 2008. Growth in Mobile Air Conditioning: A Socio-Technical Research Agenda. *Building Research and Information* 36(4): 351–362.

Phookan, M. 2004. Consumption and Cosmetics, Industry Sector Analysis. Report prepared for the Cosmetics and Personal Care Industry, Canada. Available at http://www.ic.gc.ca/eic/site/icgc.nsf/eng/home. Accessed 25 June 2005.

Pierce, James, Diane Schiano and Eric Paulos. 2010. Home, Habits, and Energy: Examining Domestic Interactions and Energy Consumption. Proceedings, CHI 2010, 10–15 April, Atlanta, GA.

Rimmer, Peter J. and Howard Dick. 2009. *The City in Southeast Asia: Patterns, Processes and Policy.* Singapore: NUS Press.

Robbins, Richard. 2004. *Global Problems and the Culture of Capitalism.* Boston: Allyn and Bacon.

Sahakian, Marlyne. 2014. *Keeping Cool in Southeast Asia: Energy Consumption and Urban Air Conditioning.* Basingstoke and New York: Palgrave Macmillan.

Schor, Juliet. 1993. *The Overworked American: The Unexpected Decline of Leisure.* New York: Basic Books.

Shove, Elizabeth. 2003. *Comfort, Cleanliness and Convenience.* Oxford and New York: Berg.

Shove, Elizabeth and Dale Southerton. 2000. Defrosting the Freezer: From Novelty to Convenience: A Narrative of Normalization. *Journal of Material Culture* 5(3): 301–319.

Shove, Elizabeth and Alan Warde. 2002. Inconspicuous Consumption: The Sociology of Consumption, Lifestyles and the Environment. In Riley E. Dunlap, Frederich H. Buttel, Peter Dickens and August Gijswijt (eds), *Sociological Theory and the*

Environment: Classical Foundations, Contemporary Insights. Plymouth: Rowman and Littlefield, pp. 230–252.

Smith, Adrian. 2007. Translating Sustainabilities between Green Niches and Socio-technical Regimes. *Technology Analysis and Strategic Management* 19(4): 427–450.

Smith, Virginia. 2007. *Clean: A History of Personal Hygiene and Purity*. Oxford: Oxford University Press.

SSB. 2014. Dette er Norge 2014. Report published by the National Bureau of Statistics, Norway, 14 July.

Urry, John. 2004. The 'System' of Automobility. *Theory, Culture and Society* 21(4/5): 25–39.

US Department of Energy. 2009. Refrigerator Market Profile: New Opportunities Multiply Savings. December. Available at http://apps1.eere.energy.gov/states/pdfs/ref_market_profile.pdf. Accessed 10 April 2015.

US Energy Information Administration. 2012. *2012 Annual Energy Review*. Washington DC: US Department of Energy.

Veblen, T. 1899. *The Theory of the Leisure Class: An Economic Study of Institutions*. New York: Macmillan.

Wallenborn, G. and H. Wilhite. 2014. Rethinking Embodied Knowledge and Household Consumption. *Energy Research and Social Science* 1: 56–64.

Weber, Chrisotpher and H. Scott Matthews. 2007. Embodied Environmental Emissions in U.S. International Trade, 1997–2004. *Environmental Science and Technology* 42(10): 3508–3513.

Whitelegg, J. 1997. *Critical Mass: Transport Environment and Society in the Twenty-First Century*. London: Pluto Press.

Wilhite, H. 2008. *Consumption and the Transformation of Everyday Life: A View from South India*. Basingstoke and New York: Palgrave Macmillan.

Wilhite, H. 2009. The Conditioning of Comfort. *Building Research and Information* 37(1): 84–88.

Wilhite, H. 2012. The Energy Dilemma. In K. Bjørkdahl and K. B. Nielsen (eds), *Development and the Environment: Practices, Theories, Policies*. Oslo: Universitetsforlaget, pp. 81–99.

Wilhite, H. 2014. The Body in Consumption: Perspectives from India. In D. Southerton and A. Ulph (eds), *Consumption: A Multidisciplinary Point of View*. Oxford: Oxford University Press.

Witkowski, T. H. 2010. A Brief History of Frugality Discourses in the United States. *Consumption Markets and Culture* 13(3): 235–258.

4 Mainstream green economy models for low carbon transformation

Growth, efficiency and marketization have been at the heart and soul of capitalist-driven economic development. As elaborated in the previous chapters, these drivers of capitalism are the sources of energy-related environmental problems, including climate gas emissions. Ironically, they are also at the heart of mainstream solutions for low carbon transformation. I will argue in this chapter that what has been heralded as 'green economy' in both national and international strategies to deal with climate change does not consist of much more than tinkering with economic business as usual. Neither UN initiatives on climate nor national strategies anywhere in the rich Organisation for Economic Co-operation and Development (OECD) countries seriously question growth, privatization or market economics. The UN encourages increased taxation and other fiscal policies to address climate change (UNEP 2014), but international development organizations such as the World Bank and International Monetary Fund continue to impose conditions that restrict the role of government and deregulate markets. In both international and national low carbon policies, the thinking continues to be that unfettered markets are capable of leading a low carbon transformation through greater energy efficiency and a shift to renewable energies. The persistence of this thinking denies the evidence of the past half century, in which efficiency gains in the production and consumption of energy are repeatedly overwhelmed by the added energy needed to fuel economic growth, product turnover and private accumulation.

After introducing the concept of green economy, I will discuss ecological modernization and the merging of focus on market and technological efficiency in conventional green economy and green energy programmes. I will then discuss the efforts to apply market economics to low carbon transformation through the creation of carbon markets, giving attention to the Clean Development Mechanism (CDM), a market for carbon emission permits, and the United Nations programme entitled Reducing Emissions from Deforestation and Forest Degradation (UN REDD), which commodifies forests in developing countries and credits investments in carbon sinks from rich countries with carbon reduction in their national carbon accounting. Sunita Narain (2009), Director of the Centre for Science and Environment in India, refers to these as 'creative carbon accounting' that shift the responsibility for carbon reductions from the heaviest polluters in the global north and have negative impacts on livelihoods of forest dwellers in countries of the global south. Finally, I will examine eco-motivated critiques of green economy models and their perspectives on what is needed to restore ecosystems and reduce carbon emissions.

Ecological modernization

David LeBlanc (2011) reviews the historical development of the concept of green economy and suggests that it was first introduced by David Pearce, Anil Markandya and Edward Barbier in their book published in 1989, *Blueprint for a Green Economy*. The central points of the 'blueprint' were that environmental assets, services and consequences are all either undervalued or omitted in economic systems and their associated costs left unpaid by producers. The green economy correction for this undervaluing is to be accomplished by putting a price on environmental disturbances and thus 'internalizing' the environmental costs of production and consumption in the market price. Another thrust within green capitalism has been the development of a technology-grounded theory of greening production and consumption that refers to itself as ecological modernization (Spaargaren and Mol 1992; Huber 2007). As Huber (2007: 360) formulated the concept, ecological modernization is essentially a 'readaptation of industrial society within the global geo- and biosphere by *modern means* such as a scientific knowledge base and advanced technology in order to upgrade the earth's carrying capacity and make development more sustainable'. Ecological modernization has formed the basis for both international and national policies for reducing carbon and energy and has been integrated into national 'green energy' programmes and many 'green city' programmes. These efforts have emphasized sustainable resource management, clean and energy-efficient technologies, benign substitution of hazardous substances, product design that includes environmental concerns, extended producer responsibility (or its cognate corporate social responsibility), recycling, low-emission production processes, and add-on purification technologies in emission control and waste processing. Herman Daly introduced the concept of ecosystem services into green economy approaches, putting forward the idea that eco-system preservation will bolster efforts to sustain the economy. According to Castree (2008), attention to ecosystem services has been effective in curtailing environmental degradation in many domains, including fisheries, mineral resources, water, sewage, ecosystems such as wetlands, public forests, genetic materials of animals, insects and plants, and pollution rights. However, climate change does not fit well into this ecosystem service model because carbon and other climate-gas emissions emanate from virtually every form of economic and social activity and the consequences are complex and difficult to represent in purely economic terms.

Ecological modernization and other versions of green economy are, according to Australian sociologist Ariel Salleh (2010: 137):

> A crude blend of neoliberal economics, technological innovation, and environmental sentiment…an amalgam of actual and imaginary interactions

between the financial capital, human capital, and natural capital...The ecosystem services idea commodifies nature, converting living ecosystems into a raw materials warehouse...When marketized, the exchange value of products such as medicinal herbs, foods (coffee, bananas) and energy sources (carbon, dammed rivers) is based on what it has in common with other commodities (the labour needed to produce it).

In this perspective, Salleh writes, 'dead matter (extracted from life giving biological relations) is transformed by dead labour (alienated and technologized) and distributed for consumption as dead product' (2010: 137). In a more mildly worded critique, another Australian, Clive Hamilton (2010: 573) writes that ecological modernization embraces an 'instrumentalist attitude to the natural world'. The environment is regarded as a source of 'resources...that have value only to the extent that they contribute to human welfare measured by market activity...It understands the exploitation of the natural world as not just a right but virtually a duty.'

With a few exceptions, including Herman Daly, ecological modernization theorists do not see economic growth as a problem, but rather as a part of the solution to reducing environmental consequences of human activity (see Gibbs 2006 and Baker 2007). Some of its proponents propose that growth is not merely compatible with the environment but actually capable of enhancing it, the argument being that growth will provide the capital to address environmental problems (Hajer 1995). An early critic of ecological modernization, David Pepper (1998: 5), labelled the resulting environmental policies as 'market environmentalism', characterized by weak regulatory approaches and dependent on voluntarism from the corporate sector. Robertson (2004) and others have shown how ecological modernization has been seamlessly incorporated into corporate rhetoric and into global development institutions without significantly changing practices.

According to Barry (2007), the countries that have accomplished the most from an application of the ecological modernization approach to energy and carbon policy are Germany, the Netherlands, Sweden, Japan, Great Britain and the European Union as a whole (see also Weale 1992 and Dryzek 1997). Yet none of these ambitious efforts to green the economy have aimed at reducing economic growth and all of them are explicit about not attempting to limit overall levels of production and consumption. Barry (2007: 450) writes this about Great Britain's interpretation of green economy:

> The notion that orthodox economic growth, employment and investment patterns and the cross-sectoral goals of sustainable development might be in serious tension is excluded from the government's rhetoric on the environment and the 'greening of the economy'; it is certainly not presented as a possibly problematic issue for industrial production processes or for global capitalism or the new orthodoxy of export-led growth. Instead, environmental protection and economic growth are portrayed as a positive-sum game, a 'business opportunity'.

Davies and Mullin raise a similar critique of Ireland's version of 'smart green economy', writing that the emphasis is 'on encouraging technological eco-innovation and enterprise within the private sector; that is effectively greening the outputs of the mainstream economy rather than anything more radical. As such the processes of transition to a greener economy are seen to be predominantly technical and financial rather than social or political' (2011: 794). Bluhdorn and Welsh summarize these and other efforts to incorporate ecological modernization into national political economies as toothless, writing that they have 'rehabilitated the ecologist enemies and made technological innovation, economic growth, capital accumulation and consumerism in principle acceptable – if only they were of the correct, i.e. of the "green" variety'. They go on to write that 'Green economy gives a green light signaling the continuation – if in modified form – of established practices and principles'(2007: 194).

Green energy

'Green energy' programmes in the rich and 'emerging' countries of the world conform largely to the principles of green economy and ecological modernization. They base themselves on a two-pronged strategy for reducing energy consumption and decarbonizing energy production: 1) a transformation of production from fossil fuel-based to renewable-based energy sources and 2) a reduction in the energy intensity of the economy through increased economic and technical efficiency. More weight has been given to the development of renewable energies in part because a change in energy production can be seamlessly incorporated into an economic growth strategy. This has been understood very well by China. It has made massive investments in developing, producing and marketing both solar energy and wind energy (Knutsen and Ou 2015). However, early predictions about falling prices for solar energy production have proven overly optimistic (see Guardian 2015), and high costs as well as other issues such as the pollution associated with battery and solar cell production, as well as difficulties with energy storage and producing electricity at scale are slowing the transition to solar. Recent reports of the International Energy Agency (IEA, an arm of the OECD) have predicted a slow integration of renewable energies into production portfolios over the next century and that renewable substitution will not make a significant difference to the aggregate global carbon emissions over the next half century. As I write in Wilhite (2012: 85), another major hindrance to the development of renewable energies is 'competition with coal-based energy production: coal production technologies are mature, coal reserves are plentiful and production is cheap compared to the alternatives'. Furthermore, the coal industry is provided with heavy government subsidies. According to Mason (2015), USD 544 billion are spent each year on fossil fuel subsidies. Referring to the IEA (2013) report on the progress towards reducing CO_2 emissions, Geels (2014: 36) writes that 'Despite climate change debates and policies, coal's relative contribution to electricity generation expanded from 39 per cent in 2000 to 42 per cent in 2010. Renewable electricity sources have so far been mainly *additional* (original emphasis) to fossil fuels with no (or limited) substitution effects'. Adding reserves of oil and gas to those of coal, it is estimated that there are 2.8 trillion tons of carbon reserves globally and both exploration for new reserves and production of oil from tar sands, fracking and deep sea oil deposits continues at a high tempo. In 2011, global investments in fossil fuel exploration and development was USD 674 billion (Mason 2015).

If one accounts for the slow transition to renewable energy production over the next century, as well as the post-Fukushima scepticism to nuclear energy, the implication is that a rapid reduction in carbon emissions will not happen without an absolute reduction in energy consumption in all sectors of the economy, including the residential sector, which continues to be the fastest growing energy-using sector globally. This is where the theories that inform green policy are at their weakest, ignoring the high energy habits that have formed in transport, heating, cooling, cleaning, food and other household practices. The policy emphasis remains rigidly tied to reducing energy use through the promotion of technical and economic efficiency. The theory that efficiency alone can reduce energy in a growth economy is, in the words of Wilhite and Norgard (2004) a 'delusion' in energy policy, or as formulated by Bluhdorn (2007: 80), an exercise in 'energy metaphysics'. Energy use is the product of intensity (the inverse of efficiency) and volume, but the latter is ignored in green energy policy. The delusion is evident in the historical record of efforts to reduce (or conserve) energy in the OECD countries. Over the 40 years from the birth of energy conservation, economic growth has outstripped energy efficiency, the result being small decreases in energy use for the OECD as a whole from very high starting points relative to the remainder of the world.

One has to look back to the 1980s to find the strongest political challenges to growth from an environmental perspective (Meadows et al. 1978 and the WCED 1987). The brief attention to 'limits' to growth and reduction of energy use withered in the early 1990s in the face of the wave of deregulation and, in some countries, privatization of energy utilities in North America and Europe and the establishment of so-called competitive markets for electricity, which according to its proponents would self-regulate energy savings. In the USA the deregulation was preceded by heavy marketing and political lobbying by the electricity utility industry and in particular two interest organizations, the National Rural Electric Association and the American Public Power Association, the latter consisting mainly of wealthy investor-owned utilities. The record shows that this market-driven efficiency has not resulted in significant reductions in energy consumption, and in some cases has led to the manipulation of electricity markets, as was the case in California in 1996 when electricity prices fluctuated rapidly, and there were shortages and blackouts in many areas (Haaland and Wilhite 1994; Wilhite 2012).

The neo-classical economic model of the consumer and consumption has been stubbornly resistant to innovation throughout this period. Consumption choices are theorized as rational choices by self-interested and economically rational agents whose decisions to consume in less energy-intensive ways are based on an evaluation of energy costs and the benefits of saving energy. Much information grounded in this theory has been in the form of deductive, reasoned arguments for the benefits of energy efficiency. 'End users' (as householders are defined in energy-efficiency programmes) would invest in building insulation, triple pane windows, efficient household appliances and other projects that would 'pay back' the added capital costs of their investment in the form of saved energy in X number of years. This form for information is solidly grounded in the rational choice model of household energy use, and as discussed in Chapter 2, totally ignores the experiential and material contributions to the stabilization of practices and the formation of habits. These epistemological delusions have persisted despite research results in project after project grounded in the non-economic social sciences (see Lutzenhiser 1993; Wilhite et al. 2000; Lutzenhiser 2014). I participated in one of the early anthropological studies of household consumption with Richard Wilk in northern California in the early 1980s (Wilk and Wilhite 1985). The study of households in middle-income families who had invested thousands of dollars in wall and ceiling insulation and other expensive energy savings projects such as triple pane windows had not taken the economically rational step of purchasing and installing inexpensive weatherstripping around leaky doors and windows, even though they were well aware of its potential energy and money-savings benefits. At that time, weatherstripping cost next to nothing (less than $5), was the subject of comprehensive information campaigns by energy utilities and was available in virtually every hardware store in the United States. Depending on the age and condition of the house, it had the potential to save up to 30 percent of energy costs per year by reducing the loss through the thermal envelope of the house of heated air in the winter and mechanically cooled air in the summer. These households had not acted as predicted by models based on economically rational actors and economically motivated actions. Our analysis showed that the principal reason for this was that bigger projects of insulating walls and installing windows were regarded by householders as improvements to the home, but weatherstripping was classified by most of them along with such boring tasks as replacing broken roof tiles or repairing a fence as a home maintenance or repair project. These home maintenance habits are beyond the purview of rational choice theory and green energy policy.

The neo-liberal wave of capitalist development from the 1980s reinforced the emphasis on market-driven efficiency. Norway and New Zealand were the first countries to deregulate their electricity systems, followed by Europe and the USA. Energy savings programmes narrowed their focus from promoting energy savings to targeting 'market barriers' mainly in the form of poor information on their economic benefits. In addition to removing the incentives for energy distributors to engage in energy consumption, deregulation virtually eliminated programmes offering subsidies, grants and low interest loans for energy efficient projects, seen as helping households over the barrier of coming up with the money (full cost or down payment) for projects that were profitable, but over the long term as the payback came from reduced energy costs (see Gately 1980; McMahon and Levine 1982; Meier and Whittier 1983).

The narrow focus on efficiency in the wake of deregulation was brought home to me at a conference in 2001, where I learned that the European Union's Energy Directorate supported efforts by air conditioner manufacturers and energy utilities to market and sell energy-efficient air conditioners to households and commercial buildings in southern Europe in places where there was little evidence of increasing demand for air conditioning (see Mebane and Presutto 2000). In the name of efficiency, the European Union supported the introduction of an energy-using comfort regime (and the formation of new habits) which would expand energy use for cooling in places with stable, non-energy-dependent cooling habits. A strategy truly interested in reducing energy use for home comfort would aim at supporting existing non-mechanical solutions for achieving comfortable and cool homes and retaining the cooling habits that had been practised for many generations, involving the use of shading, porches, ducts and fans to achieve cooling comfort. Stabilizing this cooling habit is crucial to low carbon transformation but antithetical to capitalist development; it is therefore off of the radar of green energy policies.

Smart technology

One of the new thrusts in green energy policy involves 'smart' technology, a technology-centred strategy to reduce building energy use through transferring the control of heating and cooling comfort to advanced technologies and sophisticated thermostatic controls. There is now a substantial body of evidence that smart systems do not conform to the ways people prefer to regulate comfort because they are overly complex and lead to 'sub-optimal' (from the designer perspective) behaviours by the occupants, such as opening and closing windows to regulate indoor temperatures or overriding automatic thermostat systems (Pickerill and Maxey 2009). Wade (2015) reviews studies of how people understand and use smart meters. These studies reveal that in a number of different national settings, there are many cases where the smart technologies are not being used as intended and in some cases residents are not even aware that they have smart controls (for example Rathouse and Young 2004; Woods 2006; Revell and Stanton 2014). A nationwide study from Finland revealed that over 60 percent of respondents reported that they either did not use their thermostat at all or changed its setting less frequently than once a month (Karjalainen 2007). Furthermore, in a study of houses with and without thermostat controls in the UK, Shipworth et al. (2010) found no statistical difference in average maximum living room temperatures in households with and without smart meters.

In her book entitled Smart Utopia, Australian Yolande Strengers (2013) cites evidence from a number of studies that many people are sceptical to the idea of living in a smart house and ceding control of comfort to smart technologies (Vyas and Gohn 2012); that people living in smart houses often do not use them in ways intended by designers (Valocchi and Juliano 2012); and that one of the reasons for these problems is that technology designers imagine a householder energy consumer as being much like themselves, what Strengers defines as 'resource man': a male who makes decisions for the entire household; is well educated; is interested in energy data; is techno-savvy; and responds rationally to price signals. Unfortunately, this imagined householder does not correspond to most men and women of any age, place or social class, and as Strengers points out, completely leaves out the majority of households in which both men and women participate in decision making, as well as the elderly, teenagers and low-income households.

In an ongoing study of families in Oslo living in an apartment building in which regulating heat and fresh air is dependent on mechanical ventilation, very few of the families interviewed understood the workings of the smart interface with the mechanical ventilation system or used it as designed (Standal et al. forthcoming). Ventilation is necessary because the building has a double bank of south-facing windows to capture passive solar heat. Most of the residents regulate heat and ventilate by overriding automatic thermostatic controls (manually adjusting temperature settings) and regulating fresh air by opening and closing balcony doors and windows. Most of those interviewed said they preferred to have control over (actively regulate) heat and draughts and were sceptical to the delegation of comfort regulation to automated technology. This is consistent with the findings from Wade's (2015) study of the interactions between the heat engineers who install home heating systems in the UK and the recipient households. The heat engineers found that households of all ages and socio-economic groups had difficulty understanding smart meter interfaces. They never recommend smart thermostatic controls for older people and for those households who do elect to install them, heat engineers recommend a simple method for regulating temperatures that ignore and override the complex programming required by the smart device.

In the 'smart utopia' of green energy policy, the formation of many home energy-using habits are being scripted by designers and manufacturers in ways that delegate agency from body to technology, make experimentation and control more difficult and result in sub-optimal performance (from an energy perspective) as people manually override automatic settings. There is a dire need for systems that engage with people's know-how about heating, cooling and ventilating and allow for their active engagement with comfort systems. Overly complex thermostatic heating and cooling controls are doomed to fail to achieve the projected direct energy savings.

The ghost of Jevons

One of the most widely researched consequences of the efficiency delusion is the 'rebound effect': in a growth economy the energy 'saved' through efficiency will likely be invested in other energy-using activities, thus dissipating or eliminating altogether the expected savings. This was first pointed out by Jevons, who wrote in 1866 'It is wholly a confusion of ideas to suppose that the economical use of fuel is equivalent to a diminished consumption. The very contrary is the truth' (Jevons 1866, quoted in Schneider 2010: 600). According to Alcott (2005), early twentieth century economists were cognizant of this rebound effect, but by the mid-twentieth century and the birth of the 'energy efficiency' domain of research and policy, Jevons and his paradox were put aside in energy analysis and planning. However, as study after study has demonstrated from the 1980s, the 'rebound effect' is at work, both at the level of national economy and household. The purchase and installation of a more efficient energy-using appliance (such as a car, washing machine or home heating system) make money available to the household, which may then be used to support consumption of more of the same energy service (such as transport, space heat or hot water), or to support a shift to more energy-intensive practices (Brannlund et al. 2007; Foster et al. 2010; Frondel et al. 2010; Sorrell et al. 2009).

In a recent study in Norway (Winther and Wilhite 2015), the consumption rebound effect was identified in a large sample of Norwegian households who had purchased a heat pump, a technology which in theory should reduce the consumption of household heating by 25 percent compared with conventional electric heaters, but in the studied group there was little or no change in electricity consumption (Halvorsen and Larsen 2013). Using a qualitative interview sample with households who had purchased a heat pump, Tanja Winther and I studied a sample of these households and found that many of those who had installed heat pumps had begun to heat bedrooms and other parts of the house where they had formerly maintained lower temperatures. Many others had increased the length of the heating season, turning the heat on earlier in the autumn and leaving it on later in the spring. A few had reduced their use of fuel wood and compensated this with the use of more electrically produced heat after the heat pump was installed. Thus this new energy-efficient heating technology led to a change in heating practices that resulted in a negation of the savings from the energy-efficient technology.

At the level of national energy consumption, the post-World War II energy use records of the USA and UK show clear examples of national energy rebounds. Between 1950 and 2005, the energy intensity of the US economy halved (energy use per GDP) but the total energy use tripled (Schneider 2010). The energy intensity of Great Britain's economy decreased by 40 percent from 1980 to 2008 (Jackson 2009: 69), yet energy use per capita increased over the same period. The energy intensity of the global economy is now 33 percent of what it was in 1970 yet global energy use has increased significantly. There has also been a global carbon rebound. The carbon intensity of the global economy declined by 25 percent from 1980 to 2006 (Sachs 2014), yet global carbon emissions increased by 80 percent from 1970 to 2008 and 60 percent from 1990 to 2008 (Jackson 2009).

As Barry notes in his assessment of Great Britain's Green Policy of 2005 (DEFRA 2005), 'The strategy document studiously avoids what many would see as the real issue with consumption – *i.e.*, how to reduce it rather than simply focus on making it "greener" or lessen its environmental impact' (Barry 2007: 453). The advocates of green economy would have it both ways: promote increased energy efficiency as a source of income for increased production, innovation and competitiveness on the one hand, and as a means to reduce energy use and carbon emissions on the other. This is a formula that is doomed to fail from a low carbon perspective. Energy efficiency is a means, not an end. It is important that it continue to be a goal for low energy and low carbon policy, but it will only contribute to deep reductions if it is framed in a broader set of policy goals that aim at reducing both the size of the economy and the amounts of energy used to fuel household practices.

Global carbon markets

In policies aimed at reducing or sequestering carbon, the emphasis has been placed on the use of fiscal, technological and market-liberal policies. UN REDD (Reduced Emissions from Deforestation and Forest Degradation), created in 2007, is a carbon sequestration programme with a global scope. It establishes a carbon market in which high CO_2-emitting countries can get credit for their emission-reduction commitments by paying local communities in Africa, Asia and Latin America to preserve biomass (save trees). Another global programme, the Clean Development Mechanism (CDM) was set up to reduce CO_2 emissions through trade in carbon-emission permits. Other versions of carbon trading have been established at regional and national levels, such as the European Union's Emissions Trading Scheme (see Ellerman et al. 2010). Both UN REDD and CDM involve global transfers of funds from rich countries to countries of the global south (including Asia) on the basis of assured CO_2 reduction or sequestration. Both are based on market economics and assumptions that markets for CO_2 certificates will foster decreases in emissions where they are most lucrative.

CDM creates a market for Certified Emission Reductions (CERs), each of which represents one tonne of carbon equivalents. CERs can be purchased and traded in a global market. The thinking is that reducing CO_2 emissions in the high-emitting countries has a higher marginal cost than in low-emitting developing countries, especially in rapidly developing countries such as India and China. By putting a price on carbon emissions generated in developing countries, and by linking that price with emissions-trading markets in developed countries, high-emitting countries will presumably save on their own carbon abatement costs and at the same time spur both emission reduction and investment in developing countries. CDM is also intended to encourage green 'leapfrogging' through the transference of green technologies and knowledge to developing countries.

Most analysts conclude that after 20 years CDM has had only marginal effects on global CO_2 emissions (see Boyer 2014). Empirically grounded research on CDM projects indicates that CDM funding has only made a small impact on both project financing and CO_2 reduction (see Turkanovic 2009). As Harvey (2014: 248) writes: 'What Al Gore's great gift to the environmental movement as it sought to do something about global warming was to create a new market in hedge funds but has done little to curb total global carbon emissions'. The market theory behind CDM is not working, nor are the intended outcomes being achieved in terms of reduced global carbon emissions. In her 2013 assessment of the CDM market, Clark (2013) concluded that CDM markets had 'essentially collapsed' (cited in Boyer 2014: 317).

UN REDD encompasses a wide range of international partners, including the Food and Agricultural Organization, the UN Development Program, and the UN Environmental Program (UNEP). The ideas behind UN REDD were first laid out at the UN climate change negotiations in Bali in 2007. A year later, the UN, with Norway as one of the major backers, jointly launched UN REDD. The programme is directed at stabilizing carbon sinks in the form of forest biomass. Deforestation and forest degradation release the climate gas CO_2 and at the same time diminish the future global carbon storage capacity. UN REDD awards carbon reduction credits to high CO_2-emitting rich countries in return for payment to forest communities for biomass protection. The intention is to achieve cost-effective and verifiable reductions of greenhouse gas emissions by increasing carbon storage in recipient countries. The programme is a classic example of market environmentalism, based on commodification of forest products and their insertion into a formula for global carbon reduction that awards reduction credits for carbon fixation. The rationale for the programme is that deforestation today constitutes 20 percent of global CO_2 emissions, the second-largest source of emissions after the energy sector, and that deforestation continues at an alarming rate. Between 1990 and 2005 the rate of global deforestation averaged 13 million hectares, mostly in tropical forests. It is estimated that by 2100 the clearing of tropical forests could release 87 to 130 gigatonnes of carbon to the atmosphere.

Early recipients of UN REDD funding were Tanzania, Indonesia, Bolivia, Brazil, Mexico, Vietnam, Zambia and Guyana. These countries developed national UN REDD strategies and established systems for the monitoring, assessment, reporting and verification of forest cover and carbon stocks. Brazil, one of the first countries to commit to UN REDD, already had in place a national framework for licensing forestation projects and in setting up and certifying forest management systems. These efforts in Brazil revealed uncertainties about land ownership and tenure rights. In Brazil, 25 percent of forested land is private and 35 percent is dedicated to indigenous communal territory; the remaining forested land is considered public with weakly enforced tenure laws. If these tenure issues are not taken into account, it is estimated that large landowners, who account for about 80 percent of all deforestation, will reap the highest benefits from UN REDD (Borner and Wunder 2008/2009). Another contentious issue in UN REDD concerns the setting of forest baseline, against which the success of reforesting will be measured. Agra-foresting activities such as the localizing of coffee or sugar cane plantations in or near forests are eligible for UN REDD projects. This encourages the conversion of forest lands to agribusiness and increases the pressures on indigenous peoples, as well as reducing biodiversity. The programme faces these and other challenges related to licensing projects, monitoring results, measuring outputs (in this case emission reductions), crediting investors and impacting positively on micro-economies and on the lives of people in affected areas. In Tanzania, an evaluation of the early stages of UN REDD revealed significant corruption and syphoning off of funds intended for forest communities by the Ministry of Natural Resources and Tourism (Lang 2013).

UN REDD also faces many of the same challenges as international development projects: acknowledgement of local know-how, engaging local people in the planning process and ensuring that these carbon-reduction initiatives provide incentives and benefits for people living in and around the affected areas. Millions of people live in tropical forests and depend on them for food, animal fodder, fuel wood and building materials. According to the World Commission on Forests and Sustainable Development, 350 million of the world's poorest people, among them 60 million indigenous people, depend almost entirely for their subsistence and survival on forests – while another billion people depend on forests as an important part of their livelihoods and as a safeguard against poverty. It is a major challenge to find ways of ensuring that forest communities, including indigenous peoples, can continue to harvest sustainably from the forests, or that alternative livelihoods or paths of economic development are made available to them. Any programme which tampers with forest and biomass risks upsetting the livelihoods and cultural practices of forest peoples. There has been little attention given to how UN REDD funds are affecting cultural ecology, sustainable harvesting of forest products and local agriculture.

Sunita Narain (2009), Director of the Centre for Science and the Environment in New Delhi, a research advocacy institute for both the rights of India's disenfranchised forest people and a strong 'southern' voice in global negotiations on climate and other environmental issues, had this to say about UN REDD.

> REDD, or 'reducing emissions from deforestation and forest degradation' – naturally, in developing countries – is being built with absolutely no understanding that forests here are not mere carbon sticks to beat the world's conscience with, or sinks for garbage carbon, but habitats of millions of people. There is no comprehension of the role forests play in a developing country's economy or in people's lives. Instead, the intent is misbegotten and single-minded: pay as cheaply as possible to buy rights over forests in the developing world and build as many accounting and certification procedures as possible to make sure there are no 'leakages' in the transaction. It is clearly a great business for the crashed and failed consultancy companies of the western world – creative carbon accounting, this time in the forests of the poor.

One of the biggest problems with UN REDD is its lack of attention to the main source of forest degradation in Asia and Latin America, namely commercial activities that use forest ecosystems as resources for their extractive activities, such as mining, logging (both legal and illegal), soft drink bottling, energy projects (such as hydropower plants and coal), agribusiness, commercial livestock grazing and pharmaceutical companies (Pacheco et al. 2010). In Latin America less than 6 percent of deforestation is attributed to local agriculture or gathering of fuelwood. Local people get some benefit from commercial extractive activities, such as salaried work, but the main benefits go to investors and stockholders. The thinking behind UN REDD reflects the paradigmatic flaw in low carbon transformations of all varieties: reducing carbon within a regime that supports economic growth and the interests of capital.

In her article from 2010 entitled 'Climate Strategy: Making the Choice between Ecological Modernization or Living Well', Ariel Salleh is sharply critical of programmes that extend the global reach of ecological modernization such as CDM and UN REDD. She argues that the consequence is

> the assimilation of communities to the capitalist economic system (and that) the UNEP's Global Green New Deal of 2008 is essentially a 'development' model where people become 'human capital' and their habitat is quantified as 'natural capital'. By this reckoning, common land, water, biodiversity, labour, and loving relationships are pulled away from an autonomous web of eco-sufficiency...Through the lens of green economy, nature is dead, merely a 'raw materials warehouse'. It is therefore no surprise that global climatic patterns fail, as living ecosystems are subjected to this anthropo-centric vanity...The North's ecological modernization approach to sustainable development serves mainly to advance international capital.
>
> (Salleh 2010: 119)

These market-based strategies for dealing with climate change extend rather than challenge the same mechanisms that have brought the global society to the brink of irreversible environmental damage: growth and market fundamentalism. By crediting rich, high-emitting countries with carbon reduction through investments elsewhere, they reduce pressure to reduce domestic carbon emissions. They represent an extension of the problem at the core of green economy models which put the sustainability of capitalism first and the reduction of energy and carbon second.

Circular economy but intended to spiral upward

Circular economy is the most recent within-capitalism innovation intended to green the economy. It promotes product prolongation and the increased recycling of materials, arriving at what is conceptualized as a circular economy, intended to decrease the extraction of natural resources and waste (Tukker 2013). The concept was first operationalized in China in the 1980s, related to efforts to alleviate the problem of excessive consumption of raw materials due to rapid economic growth (Zhijun and Nailing 2007). Improving the environmental impact of economic activity was one of the original aims of circular economy in China, but according to Zhijun and Nailing, over time the goals of circular economy have been transformed and today it has emerged as an economic strategy intended to free up capital for economic growth.

Over the past decade, the European Union has committed to moving towards a circular economy; however, there is evidence that the same inversion of goals that has taken place in China is evident in European circular economics, and that the benefits of the circularity are regarded first and foremost as contributors to economic competitiveness and growth rather than to environmental amelioration. The European Union webpage reference to circular economy puts economic activity first and waste reduction second, expressing the goals of the circular economy as 'boosting business, reducing waste' (European Union 2015). In 2014, the EU commissioned a study of the problems and benefits of the circular economy by the Ellen MacArthur Foundation (2015), the findings of which almost exclusively premier improvements to the economy, rather than the environment. For example, the study highlights the finding that a circular economy could yield an improved European economic growth rate of 11 percent to 2030 compared to current projections of 4 percent.

A number of studies point to flaws in the energy-saving predictions of circular economy models. Bianchi and Birtwistle (2012) argue that the emphasis on recycling will discourage efforts to make products more durable and encourage more rapid product turnover. Andersen et al. (2007) suggest that the energy-saving benefits of recycling diminish as materials degrade, thus limiting product circularity. Prendeville et al.'s (2014) analysis indicates that the mineral ores that are important to the production of many energy-intensive metals are difficult to recover and reuse. Still, the most important criticism from a low-carbon perspective is that in this and the other variations on green economy discussed in this section, including ecological modernization, carbon trading and carbon sequestration, the carbon, energy and other resources saved are allowed (or intended) to be fed back into the growth economy, dampening or eliminating the positive carbon-reduction and environmental impacts.

Eco-motivated critiques of green economy

Ariel Salleh is one of a number of critics of green economy from the academic disciplines that qualify their disciplinary perspective with the adjective environmental or ecological; examples are ecological economics, environmental economics, environmental sociology and environmental anthropology. Many of the emerging perspectives from these disciplines challenge one or more of the principles of capitalist political economy: economic growth, private ownership, product longevity, fiscal reductionism and individualization; however, very few of these critiques characterize capitalism as the problem or argue for a systemic change in the political economy of capitalism. Furthermore, few engage with the habits of capitalism or the issues of breaking and changing habits. In the remainder of this section I review representative low-carbon prescriptions from ecological economics and other ecologically oriented social sciences, then explore more radical ecological critiques that regard capitalism as the problem rather than the solution.

Ecological economics is the branch of economics that reverses the usual relationship between economy and ecology, putting the health of the ecology first and attempting to structure a viable economy accordingly. Many of its proponents critique the proposition that the environment can be sustained within a growth economy. The words of Prugh et al. (2000: 18) encapsulate the critique:

> Because economic production is basically the process of converting the natural world...to the manufactured world (houses, cars, computers, roads, books, plastic toys, etc., and non-natural ecosystems such as parks and fields), the economy can grow only at the expense of the global ecosystem...Since no subsystem can outgrow its host, the economy cannot grow larger than the global ecosystem...This leads inescapably to the most important idea in ecological economics: *Economic growth cannot continue indefinitely.* (original emphasis)

This critique of growth from an environmental perspective extends back to the 1970s and the writings of Herman Daly. He pointed out the immensity of the impact of human economic activity on the earth: humans use up 40 per cent of the earth's plant growth, half of the usable fresh water and disturb the chemical cycles that sustain the earth's ecosystems, including those of carbon, nitrogen and phosphorous. In his book *Steady State Economics*, Daly (1999) proposed that a 'steady state' economy could be achieved with minimal population growth, 'stable' stocks of capital and minimal material throughput. The influential publication *Limits to Growth* by Meadows et al. (1978) was also important in drawing attention to the ecosystem consequences of unlimited growth. These perspectives were widely discussed in both academic and political circles in the early 1980s. Both contributed to an acknowledgement that economic development must take on board the necessity for sustaining the environment, encapsulated in the concept 'sustainable development'.

These new ideas about the relationship between economic development and the environment were pushed onto the international political agenda by the 'Brundtland Report' (WCED 1987) and the book based on the report, *Our Common Future*. Within a few years of its publication, however, concern about the paradigmatic reversal of economic and environmental sustainability prompted the replacement of sustainable development with 'sustainable growth', a crucial difference that weakened the impact of environmental concerns and supported the milder 'green economy' models discussed above. One of the many examples of the appropriation of sustainable development by conventional political economy is cited in Victor (2008: 20). He writes that in 2007, the Canadian Department of Finance defined sustainable development as 'long term sustainable economic growth based on environmentally sound policies and practices. Environmental degradation at the local, national and international level undermines prospects for continued economic development.' In other words, development should not be redefined to support and protect the environment, but the environment should be protected to support and protect the capacity of the economy to grow.

Voices from the ecologically oriented social sciences have critiqued this watering down of the notion of sustainable development and characterized it as a veiled support for the sustenance of the growth paradigm. More recently this ecological critique has merged with research on human wellbeing which provides evidence that life satisfaction does not increase infinitely with growth (Easterlin 1974, 2003; Layard 2005). As the work of Layard and Easterlin indicates, there is evidence that beyond a certain level of personal accumulation, wellbeing either flattens out or declines. In a book chapter in the *Global Handbook of Well-being and Quality of Life*, Guillen-Royo and Wilhite (2015: 316) review this evidence and conclude 'that people's wellbeing is determined by many factors besides the economic or material and that increased production does not necessarily result in increased wellbeing'. This broader critique of conventional economy from both ecological and wellbeing perspectives lies at the heart of critical scholarship loosely grouped under the heading of 'Degrowth' or 'Decroissance'. Degrowth scholars propose that in rich societies, economic growth is degrading the environment and not adding to quality of life. They propose a politic of downshifting and economic contraction (Latouche 2010). Schneider et al. (2010: 512) summarize the essence of the thinking behind sustainable degrowth as follows: 'Sustainable degrowth may be defined as an equitable downscaling of production and consumption that increases human well-being and enhances ecological conditions at the local and global level, in the short and long term...The paradigmatic proposition of degrowth is therefore that human progress without economic growth is possible.' The degrowth movement within academia had reached a sufficient critical mass in 2000 to convene the first conference on 'Economic Degrowth for Ecological Sustainability and Social Equity' in Paris in 2008. In the intervening years, a number of degrowth scholars have insisted on a shift away from equating economic growth with prosperity (Jackson 2009; van den Bergh 2008; Costanza et al. 2014). Jackson and Victor (2013) make the point that prosperity in its original meaning in Latin is equated with a continual quest for wellbeing and social progress and thus more appropriate as an economic goal than growth, which does not necessarily deliver either.

In several recent books and journal articles, Tim Jackson fleshes out the elements of a shift in political economy from growth to prosperity, putting emphasis on downscaling in work and productivity. According to Jackson and Victor (2013: 32), 'the conventional economic view sees work as a sacrifice of our time, leisure, and comfort; wages are a "compensation" for that sacrifice'. Jackson proposes that work should be restored to its place as an activity that gives pleasure and is organized to encourage creativity and satisfaction. One of the barriers to rethinking work in this way is the capitalist drive for labour productivity, which is the amount of output delivered (on average) by each hour of work. Jackson writes (2012) that labour productivity 'is seen as the engine of progress in modern capitalist economies...The drive for increased labour productivity occupies reams of academic literature and haunts the waking hours of CEOs and Treasury Ministers across the world'. For Jackson, the result of this obsession is more work for less pleasure and a reinforcement of the spiral in which we work in order to consume an increasing number of material goods. 'We have become accustomed to "iPhones, hybrid cars, cheap holiday flights and plasma screen TVs", promoted and accompanied by a view that "time is money". This view is behind increasing ecological problems and does not work in sectors like education and health where speed does not equate to higher quality' (Jackson 2012: 1, cited in McNeill and Wilhite 2015: 41).

Clive Hamilton argues that economic growth discourages product usefulness and encourages 'planned obsolescence...Differentiation rather than standardization now characterizes products; production decisions respond to the enormously variegated, specific and constantly changing demands of consumers so that marketing creativity has replaced production efficiency as the key to competitiveness and corporate success' (2010: 572). He suggests that 'The modern consumer has moved from asking "Do I really need a new one?" To "Why should I make do with the old one?"' (Hamilton 2010: 574). These critiques of work productivity, consumerism, product turnover and the power of marketing are summarized by Eric Ringmar (2005: 3) in his book *Surviving Capitalism: How We Learned to Live with the Market and Remained almost Human*. He writes that 'Societies are being reorganized in the image of the market. Efficiency, rationality and productivity are to characterize ever more of what we do, and what cannot be justified in such terms should disappear.'

Green economy models continue to rely on the driving forces of capitalism (growth, efficiency, rationality, productivity) in efforts to transform to low carbon. In other words, the very modes of socio-economic organization that got us into the now critical sustainability dilemmas are those that are proposed by green economy as the modes to get us out. The more radical degrowth scholars draw attention to this irony and propose a new economic vision that replaces growth, efficiency and material accumulation with prosperity, security and life quality. Still, these and other critiques from an ecological perspective are on the whole very careful about questioning capitalism as an organizing socio-economic system or even using the word capitalism in their critiques. Van den Bergh (2010) goes so far as to warn against an ecological critique that takes on capitalism because it will delegitimize the ecological perspective. He suggests that we should rather retain growth as an economic goal and redefine GDP in such a way as to include environmental amelioration and exclude pollution. 'I believe in facing reality, recognizing and accepting such diverse phenomena like greed, opportunism, status seeking and rebound, which are unlikely to be countered by altruism' (2010: 542).

'Facing reality' is used time and again as a rhetorical strategy to squash radical critiques of capitalism's anti-ecological imperatives. It is used by both well-meaning and/or institutionally conservative critiques such as those of van den Bergh; by the ecological modernists and the green energy advocates; and by the ideological proponents of capitalism who insist that an abandonment of growth, competition and free markets will lead to the devastation of industrial development, to underemployment and to economic chaos. My argument is that the 'facing reality' rhetoric can and should be turned on its head in the light of climate change and other critical ecosystem disturbances. The 'reality' is that the logic of capitalism and the habits fostered by it are causing violence to the environment. It is this reality we must face and transform. Doing so moves transforming capitalism and the high everyday habits it fosters to the heart of low carbon transformation.

References

Alcott, Blake. 2005. Jevon's Paradox. *Ecological Economics* 54(1): 9–21.

Andersen, Torben M., Bengt Holmström, Seppo Honkapohja, Sixten Korkman, Söderström Korpo, Hans Tson and Juhana Vartiainen. 2007. The Nordic Model: Embracing Globalization and Sharing Risks. Report published by the Research Institute of the Finnish Economy. Available at http://websites.rcc.edu/biancardi/files/2010/03/The-Nordic-Model.pdf. Accessed 13 August 2015.

Baker, S. 2007. Sustainable Development as Symbolic Commitment: Declaratory Politics and the Seductive Appeal of Ecological Modernisation in the European Union. *Environmental Politics* 16: 297–317.

Barry, John. 2007. Towards a Model of Green Political Economy: From Ecological Modernisation to Economic Security. *International Journal of Green Economics* 1(3/4): 446–464.

Bianchi, Constanza and Grete Birtwistle. 2012. Consumer Clothing Disposal Behaviour: A Comparative Study. *International Journal of Consumer Studies* 36(3): 335–341.

Bluhdorn, I. 2007. Democracy, Efficiency, Futurity: Contested Objectives of Societal Reform. In I. Bluhdorn and U. Jun (eds), *Economic Efficiency: Democratic Empowerment*. Lanham, MD: Rowman and Littlefield/Lexington, pp. 69–98.

Bluhdorn, Ingolfur and Ian Welsh. 2007. Eco-Politics beyond the Paradigm of Sustainability: A Conceptual Framework and Research Agenda. *Environmental Politics* 16(2): 185–205.

Borner, J. and S. Wunder. 2008/2009. Paying for Avoided Deforestation in the Brazilian Amazon: From Cost Assessment to Scheme Design. *International Forestry Review* 10(3): 496–511.

Boyer, Dominc. 2014. Energopower: An Introduction. *Anthropological Quarterly* 87(2): 309–334.

Brannlund, R., T. Ghalwash, J. Norstrom. 2007. Increased Energy Efficiency and the Rebound Effect: Effects on Consumption and Emissions. *Energy Economics* 29(1): 1–17.

Castree, Noel. 2008. Neoliberalising Nature: The Logics of Deregulation and Reregulation. *Environment and Planning* 40: 131–152.

Clark, Pilita. 2013. EU Emissions Trading Faces Crisis. *Financial Times*. Available at http://www.ft.com/cms/s/0/42e719c0-63f0-11e2-84d8-00144feab49a.html#axzz3ma woySfZ. Accessed 23 September 2015.

Costanza, R., I. Kubiszewski, E. Giovannini, H. Lovins, J. McGlade, K. E. Pickett, K. V. Ragnarsdottir, D. Roberts, R. De Vogli and R. Wilkinson. 2014. Time to Leave GDP Behind. *Nature* 505: 283–285.

Daly, Herman E. 1999. *Steady-State Economics*. Washington, DC: Island Press.

Davies, Anna R. and Sue J. Mullin. 2011. Greening the Economy: Interrogating Sustainability Innovations beyond the Mainstream. *Journal of Economic Geography* 11: 793–816.

DEFRA. 2005. *Securing the Future: Delivering UK Sustainable Development Strategy.* London: Department of Environment and Rural Affairs.

Dryzek, J. 1997. *The Politics of the Earth.* Oxford: Oxford University Press.

Easterlin, R. A. 1974. Does Economic Growth Improve the Human Lot? In P. A. David and M. S. Reder (eds), *Essays in Honour of Moses Abramovitz.* Cambridge, MA: Academic Press, pp. 89–125.

Easterlin, R. A. 2003. Explaining Happiness. *PNAS* 100(19): 11176–11183.

Ellen MacArther Foundation. 2015. Circular Economy Would Increase European Competitiveness and Deliver Better Societal Outcomes, New Study Reveals. 25 June. Available at http://www.ellenmacarthurfoundation.org/news/latest-research-reveals-more-growth-jobs-and-competitiveness-with-a-circular-economy. Accessed 12 August 2015.

Ellerman, A. Frank Denny, J. Convery and Christian D. Perthuis. 2010. *Pricing Carbon: The European Union Pricing Carbon Scheme.* Cambridge: Cambridge University Press.

European Union. 2015. Moving towards a Circular Economy. Available at http://ec.europa.eu/environment/circular-economy/index_en.htm. Accessed 5 August 2015.

Foster, J. B., B. Clark and R. York. 2010. Capitalism and the Curse of Energy Efficiency: The Return of the Jevons Paradox. *Monthly Review* 62(6). Available at http://monthlyreview.org/2010/11/01/capitalism-and-the-curse-of-energy-efficiency/. Accessed 26 April 2015.

Frondel, M., N. Ritter and C. Vance. 2010. Heterogeneity in the Rebound: Further Evidence from Germany. *Energy Economics* 34: 461–467.

Gately, D. 1980. Individual Discount Rates and the Purchase and Utilization of Energy-Using Durables: Comment. *Bell Journal of Economics* 11(Spring): 373–374.

Geels, Frank W. 2014. Regime Resistance against Low-Carbon Transitions: Introducing Politics and Power into the Multi-Level Perspective. *Theory, Culture and Society* 31(5): 21–40.

Gibbs, D. 2006. Prospects for an Environmental Economic Geography: Linking Ecological Modernisation and Regulationist Approaches. *Journal of Economic Geography* 82: 193–215.

Guardian 2015. Bill Gates Calls Fossil Fuel Divestment a 'False Solution'. Available at: http://www.theguardian.com/environment/2015/oct/14/bill-gates-calls-fossil-fuel-divestment-a-false-solution. Accessed 18 October 2015.

Guillen-Royo, Monica and Harold Wilhite. 2015. Wellbeing and Sustainable Consumption. In W. Glatzer (ed.), *Global Handbook of Well-being and Quality of Life.* Frankfurt: Springer.

Haaland, H. O. and H. Wilhite. 1994. DSM and Deregulation: Experiences from Norway. *Proceedings from the ACEEE 1994 Summer Study on Energy Efficiency in Buildings* 6: 101–110. Washington, DC: American Council for an Energy Efficient Economy.

Hajer, M. A. 1995. *The Politics of Environmental Discourse: Ecological Modernization and the Policy Process.* Oxford: Clarendon Press.

Halvorsen, B. and B. M. Larsen. 2013. How Do Investments in Heat Pumps Affect Household Energy Consumption? Discussion paper 737, Statistics Norway, Oslo.

Hamilton, Clive. 2010. Consumerism, Self-Creation and Prospects for a New Ecological Consciousness. *Journal of Cleaner Production* 18: 571–575.

Harvey, David. 2014. *Seventeen Contradictions and the End of Capitalism.* Oxford and New York: Oxford University Press.

Huber, Joseph. 2007. Pioneer Countries and the Global Diffusion of Environmental Innovations: Theses from the Viewpoint of Ecological Modernization Theory. *Global Environmental Change* 18: 360–367.

IEA. 2013. World Energy Outlook. Report by the International Energy Agency, 1 November, Paris.

Jackson, Tim. 2009. *Prosperity without Growth: Economics for a Finite Planet.* London and Washington, DC: Earthscan.

Jackson, T. 2012. The Cinderella Economy: An Answer to Unsustainable Growth?. *Ecologist* 27 July. Available at http://www.theecologist.org/blogs_and_comments/Blogs/other_blogs/1507111/the_cinderella_economy_an_answer_to_unsustainable_growth.html. Accessed 5 May 2014.

Jackson, T. and Victor, P. 2013. Green Economy at Community Scale. Report for the Metcalf Foundation, November.

Jevons, William. 1866. *The Coal Question.* London: Macmillan.

Karjalainen, S. 2007. Why Is It Difficult to Use a Simple Device: An Analysis of Room Thermostat. In A. Sears and J. Jacko (eds), *Human-Computer Interaction Handbook: Fundamentals, Evolving Technologies and Emerging Applications, Part I, HCII.* New York: Laurence Erlbaum Associates, pp. 544–548.

Knutsen, Hege and Xiaoxi Ou. 2015. Ecological Modernization and the Dilemmas of Sustainable Development in China. In Arve Hansen and Ulrikke Wethal (eds), *Emerging Economies and Challenges to Sustainability.* London: Routledge, pp. 65–78.

Lang, Chris. 2013. More Corruption Involving Norwegian REDD Funding in Tanzania? *REDD Monitor.* Available at http://www.redd-monitor.org/2013/02/06/more-corruption-involving-norwegian-redd-funding-in-tanzania/. Accessed 19 October 2015.

Latouche, Serge. 2010. Degrowth. *Journal of Cleaner Production* 18: 519–522.

Layard, Richard. 2005. *Happiness: Lessons from a New Science.* New York: Penguin.

LeBlanc, David. 2011. Introduction: Special Issue on Green Economy and Sustainable Development. *Natural Resources Forum* 35: 151–154.

Lutzenhiser, Loren. 1993. Social and Behavioral Aspects of Energy Use. *Annual Review of Energy and Environment* 18: 247–289.

Lutzenhiser, Loren. 2014. Through the Energy Efficiency Looking Glass. *Energy Research and Social Science* 1: 141–151.

Mason, Paul. 2015. *PostCapitalism: A Guide to Our Future.* London: Allen Lane.

McMahon, J. and M. Levine. 1982. Cost/Efficiency Tradeoffs in the Residential Appliance Marketplace. *Proceedings from the ACEEE 1982 Summer Study on Energy Efficiency in Buildings.* Washington, DC: American Council for an Energy Efficient Economy.

McNeill, D. and H. Wilhite. 2015. Making Sense of Sustainable Development in a Changing World. In A. Hansen and U. Wethal (eds), *Emerging Economies and Challenges to Sustainability.* London: Routledge, pp. 34–49.

Meadows, D. H., D. L. Meadows, J. Randers and W. W. Behrens. 1978. *The Limits to Growth.* Washington, DC: Potomac Associates.

Mebane, Bill and Milena Presutto. 2000. Room Air Conditioners: Consumer Survey in Italy and Spain. In P. Bertoldi, A. Ricci and A. Almeida (eds), *Energy Efficiency in Household Appliances and Lighting.* Berlin: Springer.

Meier, Alan and J. Whittier. 1983. Consumer Discount Rates Implied by Consumer Purchases of Energy-Efficient Refrigerators. *Energy: The International Journal* 8(12): 957–962.

Narain, S. 2009. 2009 Is Full of Promise. *Down to Earth.* Available at http://www.downtoearth.org.in/content/2009-full-promise. Accessed 20 August 2015.

Pacheco, Pablo, Mriel Aguilar-Støen, Jan Borner, Andres Etter, Louis Putzel and Maria del Carmen Vera Diaz. 2010. Actors and Landscape Changes in Tropical Latin America: Challenges for REDD+ Design and Implementation. Center for International Forestry Research (CIFOR) Infobrief no. 32, November.

Pearce, D. W., A. Markandya and E. Barbier. 1989. *Blueprint for a Green Economy*. New York: Earthscan.

Pepper, D. 1998. Sustainable Development and Ecological Modernization: A Radical Homocentric Perspective. *Sustainable Development* 6: 1–7.

Pickerill, Jenny and Marsh Maxey. 2009. Low Impact Development: The Future in Our Hands. Published under the Creative Commons Attribution-Non-Commercial-Share Alike 3.0 licence. Available athttp://creativecommons.org/licenses/by-nc-sa/3.0/.

Prendeville, Sharon, Chris Sanders, Jude Sherry and Filipa Costa. 2014. Circular Economy: Is It Enough? Report published by the Ecodesign Centre, Wales. Available at www.edcw.org. Accessed 10 August 2015.

Prugh, Thomas, Robert Costanza and Herman Daly. 2000. *The Local Politics of Global Sustianability*. Washington, DC: Island Press.

Rathouse, K. and B. Young. 2004. Domestic Heating: Use of Controls. Defra Market Transformation Program, United Kingdom.

Revell, K. M. A. and N. A. Stanton. 2014. Case Studies of Mental Models in Home Heat Control: Searching for Feedback, Valve, Timer and Switch Theories. *Applied Ergonomics* 45: 363–378.

Ringmar, Eric. 2005. *Surviving Capitalism: How We Learned to Live with the Market and Remained almost Human*. London: Anthem Press.

Robertson, M. 2004. The Neoliberalisation of Ecosystem Services: Wetland Mitigation Banking and Problems in Environmental Governance. *Geoforum* 35: 361–373.

Sachs, Jeffrey. 2014. From Words to Action: The Role of Technology. Presentation at the Joule seminar, Radisson Blu Plaza Hotel, Oslo, 9 September.

Salleh, Ariel. 2010. Climate Strategy: Making the Choice between Ecological Modernisation or Living Well. *Journal of Australian Political Economy* 66: 118–143.

Schneider, Francois. 2010. Book Review of John M. Polimeni, Kozo Mayumi, Mario Giampietro, Blake Alcott. 2008. The Jevons Paradox and the Myth of Resource Efficiency Improvements. *Journal of Cleaner Production* 18: 600–602.

Schneider, Francois, Giorgos Kallis, Joan Martinez-Alier. 2010. Crisis or Opportunity? Economic Degrowth for Social Equity and Ecological Sustainability. Introduction to This Special Issue. *Journal of Cleaner Production* 18: 511–518.

Shipworth, M., S. K. Firth, M. I. Gentry, A. Wright, D. T. Shipworth and K. J. Lomas. 2010. Central Heating Thermostat Settings and Timing: Building Demographics. *Building Research and Information* 40(4): 481–492.

Sorrell, S., J. Dimitropoulos and M. Sommerville. 2009. Empirical Estimates of the Direct Rebound Effect: A Review. *Energy Policy* 37: 1356–1371.

Spaargaren, G. and A. Mol. 1992. Sociology, Environment and Modernity: Ecological Modernisation as a Theory of Social Change. *Society and Natural Resources* 5(4): 323–344.

Standal, K., H. Wilhite and S. Wagø. Forthcoming. Household Practices in Low Energy Buildings: Bridging the 'Smart' Knowledge Gap. *Energy Research and Social Science*.

Strengers, Yolande. 2013. *Smart Energy Technologies in Everyday Life: Smart Utopia?* Basingstoke and New York: Palgrave Macmillan.

Tukker, A. 2013. Product Services for a Resource-Efficient and Circular Economy: A Review. *Journal of Cleaner Production* 97: 76–91.

Turkanovic, Zlata. 2009. A Critical Analysis of the Clean Development Mechanism in the Indian Wind Power Sector. Master's thesis, Centre for Development and the Environment, University of Oslo.

UNEP. 2014. Green Economy. Available at www.unep.org/greeneconomy/. Accessed 15 June 2015.

Valocci, Michael and John Juliano. 2012Knowledge Is Power: Driving Smarter Energy Usage through Consumer Education. IBM Business Report. Available at http://sma rtgridaustralia.com.au/SGA/Documents/Consumer_Behaviour_Report. Accessed30 June 2015

Van den Bergh, J. 2008. The GDP Paradox. *Journal of Economic Psychology* 30(2): 117–135.

Van den Bergh, J. 2010. Relax about GDP Growth: Implications for Climate and Crisis Policies. *Journal of Clean Production* 18: 540–543.

Victor, Peter A. 2008. *Managing without Growth: Slower by Design, Not Disaster.* Cheltenham and Northampton, MA: Edward Elgar.

Vyas, Charul and Bob Gohn. 2012. Smart Grid Consumer Survey. Boulder, CO:Pike Research.

Wade, Faye. 2015. An Ethnography of Installation: Exploring the Role of Heating Engineers in Shaping the Energy Consumed through Domestic Central Heating Systems. Thesis submitted for the degree of Doctor of Philosophy in Energy and Human Dimensions, UCL Energy Institute, Bartlett School of Environment, Energy and Resources, University College London.

WCED. 1987. *Our Common Future.* Oxford and New York: Oxford University Press.

Weale, A. 1992. *The New Politics of Pollution.* Manchester: Manchester University Press.

Wilhite, H. 2012. The Energy Dilemma. In K. Bjørkdahl and K. B. Nielsen, *Development and the Environment: Practices, Theories, Policies.* Oslo: Universitetsforlaget, pp. 81–99.

Wilhite, H. and J. Norgard. 2004. Equating Efficiency with Reduction: A Self-Deception in Energy Policy. *Energy and Environment* 15(3): 991–1011.

Wilhite, H., E. Shove, L. Lutzenhiser and W. Kempton. 2000. The Legacy of Twenty Years of Demand Side Management: We Know More about Individual Behavior but next to Nothing about Demand. In E. Jochem, J. Stathaye and D. Bouille (eds), *Society, Behaviour and Climate Change Mitigation.* Dordrect: Luwer Academic Press.

Wilk, R. and H. Wilhite. 1985. Why Don't People Weatherize Their Homes? An Ethnographic Solution. *Energy: The International Journal* 10(5): 621–630.

Winther, T. and H. Wilhite. 2015. An Analysis of the Household Energy Rebound Effect from a Practice Perspective: Spatial and Temporal Dimensions. *Energy Efficiency Journal* 8(3): 595–607.

Woods, J. 2006. Fiddling with Thermostats: Energy Implications of Heating and Cooling Set Point Behavior. *Proceedings of the 2006 ACEEE Summer Study.* Washington, DC: American Council for an Energy Efficient Economy.

Zhijun, F. and Y. Nailing. 2007. Putting a Circular Economy into Practice in China. *Sustain Science* 2: 95–101.

5 Low carbon governance from the top down

It should be clear from the discussion in previous chapters that challenging capitalism as a societally organizing system from a climate, energy or ecological perspective is a daunting exercise given its solid lock on global and national political economies in the rich countries of the world and its increasing influence on the political economies of the formerly socialist countries such as Russia, China, Vietnam, India and others (Hansen and Wethal 2014). The perceived inevitability of capitalism to dominate global economy is one reason that the main body of critique and recommendations for change from an ecological perspective accept capitalism and suggest refinements within it. Resistance to a deeper critique is bolstered by the commercial and political interests that thrive on the capitalist political structures and the regulatory schemes that are in place today. A reading of Chapter 4 shows that the European Union and many of the countries of Europe take climate change seriously and are making efforts to reduce carbon, though none of these challenge the capitalist imperatives of growth and consumerism. In the USA, where scepticism about climate change has inhibited aggressive climate-reduction policies, there is an active manufacture of doubt by corporate-supported 'think tanks' and corporate interest organizations, including those connected to the coal and oil industries.

In this chapter and the next I explore a low carbon political framework that includes a critique and re-examination of the capacity of the capitalist system to engender a low carbon transformation from top to bottom. I begin with the need to restructure research funding to encompass critical research that questions the capacity of capitalism to foster a low carbon transformation and suggests new forms for governance of production, work and consumption. I then move the focus to the democratic crisis due to widespread complacency about the social and climate consequences of capitalism and to active resistance to low carbon transformation from both elected politicians and industrial interest groups. I suggest that we can draw inspiration from historical governance transformations that happened in the face of divided social opinion and resistance, including the political actions on the environment in the 1960s when a number of aggressive laws and regulations were enacted. I also explore city-level initiatives that had their roots in Agenda 21, the UN charter signed at the World Commission on Environment and Development in 1991. In the next chapter, I explore bottom-up environmental governance, examining community initiatives that are taking aim at transforming community and household habits. I suggest that these communities and other non-localized initiatives emphasizing sharing and collaboration are challenging capitalism from the bottom up and provide an important source of knowledge on the politics of low carbon transformation.

The need for critical social science research

To begin with, the scope of funding for research on low carbon transformation is miniscule compared to funding for research on health and national security. Within the field of research on energy saving, funding for energy and carbon reductions are mainly oriented to fine tuning, rather than challenging capitalism. There has been a steady decrease in funding over the past couple of decades for non-tied (free) energy research and an increase in funding for projects that support the growth of the economy and the competitiveness of commercial and industrial organizations. Concerning the research councils with which I am most familiar in the European Union and Norway, funding for both basic and applied research is saturated with criteria that the keep research focus on 'relevant' research, meaning research that serves the dual purpose of reducing energy use and carbon emissions while at the same time contributing to economic growth and competitiveness. This makes it very difficult to acquire funding for projects that challenge economic business-as-usual.

Within the research domains that aim at energy and the reduction of climate emissions, projects framed by epistemologies grounded in conventional economic models have a much greater chance of receiving funding. An evaluation in 2010 of the Norwegian Research Council's funding for research on climate mitigation found that only 3 percent of funding had been granted to research projects representing the non-economic social sciences. Periodic assessments of the state of energy research over the years have pointed to the absence of socio-cultural perspectives in energy savings research and policies (Wilhite et al. 2000; Shove 2010; Moezzi and Lutzenhiser 2010). As discussed in Chapter 3, the added urgency for energy reductions from a climate change perspective and frustrations with the failure of conventional economic and technical models to deliver reductions are opening up new theoretical perspectives, including those encompassing social practices and habits, but these have not been followed up with the redirection of research funding in order to support their development. Sovacool et al. (2015) surveyed articles published in energy journals from 1999–2013 and found that less than 1 percent were authored by social scientists or humanists (including sociology, geography, history, psychology, communication and philosophy). I have no doubt that within the 1 percent of articles from a social science or humanist perspective only a very few challenge the capacity of a capitalist system to engender deep reductions in societal energy use.

These narrow research-funding policies prohibit an advancement of research and theory on energy and carbon reduction, both at the level of political economy and household. They also inhibit policy innovation and new thinking on the limitations of market environmentalism and technical efficiency to foster a deep transformation in societal energy use. It should be clear to the reader by now that my view is that a deep reduction in carbon emissions will demand a comprehensive transformation in political economy and the logics embedded in everyday notions of prosperity and progress. I agree with Hamilton when he argues 'The transition to a post-growth society will be just as far-reaching as the transition from feudalism to industrial capitalism or from industrial capitalism to global consumer capitalism. It will fundamentally transform relationships with others, our ethical rules, our attitudes to the natural environment and, ultimately, our consciousness' (2003: 205). Social and socio-ecological relationships that have been subsumed by the capitalist economy and translated into market relationships will need to be revalued and re-centred. Such a comprehensive transformation will require research that examines how these changes can be fostered at every level of governance – global, national, community and household.

Climate governance in the face of denial, division and complacency

Resistance to political action on climate change is nested within a web of denial from political and economic interests that are wary of the consequences and in many cases actively resisting change. This encourages weak and sporadic pressure from democratic constituencies to legislate aggressive policies that have the purpose of reducing energy use and climate emissions. At a deeper level there is only limited interest in comprehensive change in mature capitalist societies despite the social imbalances it has fostered. These imbalances follow in the wake of capitalist expansion. In China, India and other emerging economies, the rich are getting richer but the lower middle classes and poor are not substantially benefiting from capitalist development. Why do people in the rich capitalist countries accept maldistribution of wealth, competition, speed, long working hours, struggles to make ends meet, pollution, unhealthy products and the promise that in some distant future all of the sacrifices of the present will be justified? This question has been central to the work of social theorists such as Marx, Foucault, Gramsci and Bourdieu. Marx theorized this acceptance using his concept of fetishism, 'referring to capitalism's various masks, disguises and distortions of what is really going on around us' (Harvey 2014: 4). Foucault (1979) developed his notion of governmentality to explain how individuals internalize the discursive promises of the market society and regulate their own conduct in harmony with them. Bourdieu captured this acquiescence in the concept 'symbolic violence'. In one of his typically complex, but insightful formulations, he writes (1998: 170):

> Symbolic violence is the coercion which is set up only through the consent that the dominated cannot fail to give to the dominator (and therefore to the domination) when their understanding of the situation and relation can only use instruments of knowledge that they have in common with the

dominator, which, being merely the incorporated form of the structure of the relation of domination, make this relation appear as natural; or, in other words, when the schemes they implement in order to perceive and evaluate themselves or to perceive and evaluate the dominators...are the product of the incorporation of the (thus neutralized) classifications of which their social being is the product.

This concept of symbolic violence is a derivative of Bourdieu's broader theory of habitus discussed in Chapter 3. Applied to capitalist-oriented societies, a pervasive, collectively supported myth has penetrated individual ideas and practices: present sacrifices and injustices are justified because the good life is just around the corner. Societal relations based on this promise are internalized and shape the individual's sense of 'reality' (Hernandez 2012: 4). Burawoy uses the metaphor of chess to illustrate Bourdieu's theory of symbolic violence. He writes that in the same way that a chess player cannot play chess and at the same time question the rules, a labourer cannot question why he must work for less than the true value of his work and keep his employment. As Burawoy puts it, 'the bodily inscription of social structure as a habitus is so at home with domination that (the laborer) does not recognize it as such' (Burawoy 2011: 22).

Transformational political efforts ignore 'the extraordinary inertia which results from the inscription of social structures in bodies, for lack of a dispositional theory of practices. While making things explicit can help, only a thoroughgoing process of countertraining, involving repeated exercises, can, like an athlete's training, durably transform habitus' (Bourdieu 1998: 172). It is important to note that Bourdieu differentiated habitus according to social class, and in the case of capitalist social organization, the capitalists and political interests that support them are more reflexive about the myths and are active in upholding them. A crucial point is that any effort to do something to eliminate capitalism's social and environmental violence is impeded by the individuals and institutions who are most interested in perpetuation of the system that benefits them.

Bourdieu's concepts of habitus and his thoughts on resistance to symbolic violence have been criticized for being rigid and overly determinative. I would argue that they nonetheless contain a valuable insight into why capitalism continues to be the unchallenged socio-economic system for generating prosperity and wellbeing despite its inability to cope with environmental degradation, deep divisions in wealth, and stressed everyday lives. Despite the growing academic critique of the growth imperative and despite the increasing evidence of the ecosystem consequences of top-down, business-as-usual economics, there are few signs that middle classes either in the mature capitalist countries or in the 'emerging' economies are demanding change (this point is developed in McNeill and Wilhite 2015). There are social, ecological and religious movements that are actively arguing for climate change transformation and there is evidence that their messages are getting increasing purchase in media and public debates (see Klein 2014); and, as I will explore in the next chapter, the fundamentals of capitalist economy and social organization are being challenged from both environmental and social perspectives at the level of neighbourhood, village and community in many parts of the world, both real and virtual, where people are experimenting with how to reduce carbon footprints while maintaining or improving wellbeing and life quality. These constitute efforts to deconstruct and remake both political economy and habits and in so doing redefine human–environment relations. While many of them operate outside conventional political infrastructures, others aim to change community or city politics. Despite their heterogeneity in organization, goals and methods of setting about to accomplish change, many of these local transformative movements are linking into networks that increase their potential to impact on national and regional political economy. There needs to be increased top-down support for change in local communities and collectivities, where there are many positive signs that people are willing to work together to change habits. But given the acceleration of climate change, the climate cannot wait for these bottom-up, community-based movements to erode capitalism from below. New laws and regulations will be needed that aim at reduction in energy and material use, favouring technologies and building infrastructures that enable low energy living.

Governing the synergies of production, provision and consumption

As the examples of high energy habits discussed in Chapters 3 and 4 reveal, consumption, production and provision are related in important ways. This is neglected in neo-classical demand theory, which assigns full agency in consumption to consumers and neglects the contributions of producers and product provisioners to the constellation of products made available for consumption (Fine 2002). Consumption happens at the interface between producers and the consumers, both of who are incentivized to expand in a capitalist economy (Wilhite et al. 2000). The policies and processes of production, provision and consumption are saturated with incentives, infrastructures and technologies that are designed for high and increasing energy use. In order to enable low energy habits, the politics of a low carbon transformation will need to reregulate all three of these domains and provide incentives for low energy choices that go against the grain of capitalist development: for example, enabling the use of non-motorized transport such as walking and cycling by redesigning cities; providing more compact living spaces; designing and buildings that can be cooled without central air conditioning, buildings capable both of retaining heat (tight structures) and being properly ventilated; enabling a food system that is less refrigeration-dependent and which has a place for local markets, urban gardening and organic foods.

Making these transformations is not only dependent on government policies, but on reorienting incentive structures for designers of cities, transport systems and buildings. The challenges for building design are discussed by Pettersen (2015). She examines how eco-designers who are trained to design for low environmental impact are trapped into the logics of capitalism. Eco-design takes a product lifecycle perspective, attempting to reduce the environmental impacts of building design and construction from resource extraction, through the supply chain and throughout the lifetime of the building. Still, eco-design is a

> profit driven strategy in which efforts typically are geared at fulfilling consumer 'need', catering to demand or providing benefits while lowering impacts in the supply chain and throughout the product lifecycle...the needs 'fulfilled' and the benefits and services produced or delivered are not questioned. The goal is rather the improvement in the efficiency of this service delivery.
>
> (2015: 2)

There are no incentives for eco-design firms with business strategies built on designing, producing or marketing low-tech designs that are durable and attractive (referred to as 'sufficiency' rather than 'efficiency' designs in the industrial ecology literature, see Tukker et al. 2010 and Hargreaves et al. 2013). Another point made by Pettersen (2015) is that designers, who have mainly technical education and training, 'are not equipped to understand human activity'. Designers need to be made cognizant of household habits and practices if they are to produce designs for buildings and the systems within them that people are comfortable with and are capable of mastering. Wallenborn is an advocate of this practical learning perspective in designer–user interaction, arguing that people should be drawn into work with designers on the design of home appliances and thermostats (correcting for the problems with thermostatic design discussed in Chapter 4). An example of this is an ongoing project in Brussels, where a block of houses is being renovated with the contribution of project managers, design specialists and the inhabitants, who have shown an interest in sharing spaces and gardens (Wallenborn and Wilhite 2014b). Public policy could contribute to this by providing funding, fiscal incentives and access to this type of participant design aimed at setting the stage for low energy practices. This approach is in line with the arguments of Shove and Walker (2010) on the need for bottom-up, 'reflexive governance' in the fostering of systemic socio-technical change (formulated by Seyfang and Smith 2007 as 'niche management').

Practical learning has been important to the growing urban food movements in Europe and the USA. The number of community-supported agricultural programmes grew rapidly in the USA from an estimated 1,700 in 2005 to about 6,500 in 2012 (McFadden 2012). A study of these by Carfagna et al. (2014) revealed that public support, especially in the form of the provision of space for gardens, is important, and that the participants are motivated by ecological considerations, but that the most important facet of popularity and growth in membership is the opportunities provided to learn by doing through participation with others. Smith (2010) found that the growth of organic food consumption in the United Kingdom could be attributed to the coordination of national policies and the provision of settings for practical learning for both producers and consumers of organic food. According to Smith organic farming was marginal until the 1990s. There were only 100 organic farmers in the UK in 1980. In the early 1990s, the government supported research in organic farming and provided grants to help conventional farmers convert to organic farming. Agricultural colleges were incentivized to introduce organic food courses. Networks were established for the sharing of practical experiences. By 2007, annual organic food sales exceeded 1 billion pounds sterling. 'The organic movement transformed into an organic industry' (Smith 2010: 442). Food corporations began to make conventional products organically, including convenience foods such as frozen meals and fizzy drinks. Smith writes that while the organic food industry has grown rapidly – land farmed organically increased from 8,000 hectares in 1987 to 700,000 hectares in 2003 – only 4 percent of farmed land is organic land and only 1.7 percent of household expenditure on food is on organic products. A strong set of policies regulating food production and consumption and encouraging practical learning opportunities will be needed to sustain the momentum.

Governing work and rethinking the currency of labour and consumption

The nature and accomplishment of work in capitalist societies is related to the habits of consumption in important ways. The most obvious is that salaried work provides the currency for consumption: money. I will return to problems raised by using money as a medium for exchange below. Another facet of work in a capitalist enterprise is that work is divided into leadership, management and wage labourers. Leaders and managers are salaried but in many types of enterprises are also paid in stock options and bonuses correlated with profit, reinforcing their incentive to support company growth and profit generation. In the Organisation for Economic Co-operation and Development (OECD) countries the companies, their managers and their workers are subject to regulations on minimum wages, workplace conditions and the length of working hours, and with a few exceptions (such as the Nordic countries), working weeks are long and time off for vacations, holidays and sick leave is limited. Companies demand long working weeks and workers and their unions accede to this because they provide income to support household food, education and health purchases, but also the income to purchase and maintain household furnishings, appliances and cars that have come to be essential to accomplishing the tasks of everyday life in the limited time workers have away from work. More time at work means less time at home, and as we saw in Chapter 3, this in turn creates a demand for home appliances that can provide relief from time pressures in accomplishing household tasks. Long workdays reduce not only time for leisure, but also time to accomplish household chores, incentivizing the purchase of time-saving and energy-using appliances.

As I discussed in Chapter 4, reducing the volume of work and time dedicated to it would, as Jackson (2009) and others have argued, alleviate the time squeeze and energy used to accommodate demands on work productivity and long working hours, as well as spreading the total workload among a greater number of workers. It would also reduce energy use by reducing what Schor (1992) refers to as 'work-and-spend' cycles, in which there is a tendency to translate labour productivity into increases in production and consumption rather than increases in leisure (Ehrhardt-Martinez et al. 2015: 106). A study of the relationship between working hours and climate emissions in OECD countries by Knight, Rosa and Schor (2013) showed that longer working hours were correlated with higher emissions.

Work in the most liberal of the capitalist societies, the USA, is not accompanied by significant worker benefits in the form of vacations, pregnancy leave, health insurance or free education. According to the US Bureau of Labor Statistics, full-time workers work on average 42.7 hours per week, have on average 11.6 days of paid vacation each year and only 11 percent of employees in the private sector have paid pregnancy leave of any duration. While European countries have laws regulating shorter working weeks, longer vacations and paid pregnancy leave, there are no examples of capitalist countries aiming at major reductions to less than 30 work hours per week for fully employed workers. In many countries there is a tendency to allow or encourage a growth in part-time employment, but this does not provide sufficient income to part-time workers for basic living expenses, nor is it accompanied by job security, health and other benefits. Even the more ambitious sustainable community movements cannot do much about reducing the working hours of their participants because many of the members of these communities work in public or corporate jobs, in which salaries and working hours are fixed by the employers. A change in national guidelines will be needed in which working hours are reduced and the minimum wage increased. In the United Kingdom, the New Economics Foundation (NEC) has proposed a working week of 21 hours, based on distributing the number of hours of paid work by employed workers in the United Kingdom over the entire adult population. As Anna Coote and colleagues (Coote et al. 2013) of the NEC writes,

> A 'normal' working week of 21 hours could help to address a range of urgent, interlinked problems: overwork, unemployment, over-consumption, high carbon emissions, low well-being, entrenched inequalities, and the lack of time to live sustainably, to care for each other, and simply to enjoy life…The challenge is to break the power of the old industrial clock without adding new pressures, and to free up time to live sustainable lives.

New governance guidelines that aim to reduce work would bring comprehensive societal and environmental benefits and set the stage for experimenting with new habits that depend less on commercial energy and carbon. This transformation would be consistent with the insightful views of Polanyi on work in market economies made many years ago:

> Labor is only another name for a human activity which goes with life itself, which in its turn is not produced for sale but for entirely different reasons,

nor can that activity be detached from the rest of life, to be stored or mobilized...to separate labor from other activities of life and subject it to the laws of the market was to annihilate all organic forms of existence and replace them by a different type of organization, an atomist and individualistic one.

(1957, cited in Harvey 2014: 56)

An interesting development in many of the intentional communities (to be discussed in more detail in the next chapter) that aim to reduce environmental impacts is their emphasis on cooperation and sharing of work and consumption, such as food growing, food preparation and shared meals. This form of collectivity invests work related to householding, family, voluntary work and care giving with value without commodifying and monetizing it. These communities have achieved increased work reciprocity, sharing and reduced the use of money and a few have invented local currencies to replace national or regional money (in the case of the Euro).

As Harvey (2014) argues market exchange on a grand scale is dependent on money, but money occludes the true value of both work and the goods we purchase with the products of our labour. When we are paid for our work in money or when we pay for goods and services with money, 'we have no idea where most of the items come from, how they were produced, by whom and under what conditions or why, exactly, they exchange in the ratios they do and what the money we use is really all about' (2014: 6). Hornberg (2014) argues in a similar vein that money obfuscates the value of work, and as the recent financial crisis has clearly demonstrated, the role of money (and money markets) is poorly understood by both economists and politicians. The futures market for debt repayment, the lack of the demand for real collateral for loans and the increased use of credit transactions and credit cards in individual exchange obfuscate the value of the objects or services exchanged. There are many efforts at the local level to restore exchanges that replace the abstraction of money and credit with direct exchange (either physical or internet-based) and in a few cases, through the substitution of national currencies with local currencies, making the sources and social biographies of products more visible (Seyfang 2009; Appadurai 1986). The use of real money is declining as the volume of credit and debit transactions grows, but money, both virtual and real, is so deeply entrenched in the exchange from global to local that it is difficult to imagine its total replacement with an alternative medium of exchange. This is one of the points on a low carbon agenda that needs greater research attention. A first step would be to catalogue and analyse the many examples of local currencies and other forms of community-based exchange around the world.

Reinventing strong environmental governance

The transformation of capitalism and its energy habits must start now, with a political vision and political action aimed at transforming work, consumption, exchange and ownership. Given the complexities of climate science, the time interval before severe consequences begin to impact and the perception that transformation will involve sacrifices to economic security and life quality, a low carbon transformation will require bold leadership. In the country with the biggest per person carbon footprint and the purest form of capitalism, the USA, there are historical examples of bold political action in the face of crisis from which we can draw inspiration. The political action resulting in the elimination of slavery in the 1800s was a transformation that had widespread economic impacts and was strongly resisted by the large segment of the population who were profiting from slavery. Another was US President Franklin Roosevelt's 'New Deal' in the 1930s and 1940s, which included the creation of federal income tax and a system of social security. US President Lyndon Johnson's 'Great Society' in 1960s created federally financed health care for the elderly and low-income families, as well as implementing bold laws and regulations on civil rights for minorities and women.

In the domain of environmental and climate-related transformation, there was a wave of important environmental laws and regulations put in place in the 1960s and 1970s. These changes followed in the wake of the first shocking evidence of the health and environmental consequences of industrial pollution (Carson 1962). Change – social, economic and environmental – was a legitimate political subject not only in the corridors of power but in homes and neighbourhoods. Positive change and social progress were taken up in many grassroots civil movements including those aimed at defeating racism, promoting women's rights and reducing industrial pollution. This widespread political acknowledgement of the environmental side effects of the post-war surge in economic growth made it possible for a candidate for president in 1968, Robert Kennedy, to articulate a new economic vision in a campaign speech in California that reassessed the relationship between life quality, economic growth and the environment (cited in Kurlansky 2004: 140):

> Too much and for too long, we seemed to have surrendered personal excellence and community values in the mere accumulation of material things. Our Gross National Product, now, is over $800 billion a year, but that Gross National Product – if we judge the United States of America by that – that Gross National Product counts air pollution and cigarette advertising, and ambulances to clear our highways of carnage. It counts special locks for our doors and the jails for the people who break them. It counts the destruction of the redwood and the loss of our natural wonder in chaotic sprawl. It counts napalm and counts nuclear warheads and armored cars for the police to fight the riots in our cities. It counts Whitman's rifle and Speck's knife, and the television programs which glorify violence in order to sell toys to our children. Yet the gross national product does not allow for the health of our children, the quality of their education or the joy of their play. It does not include the beauty of our poetry or the strength of our marriages, the intelligence of our public debate or the integrity of our

public officials. It measures neither our wit nor our courage, neither our wisdom nor our learning, neither our compassion nor our devotion to our country, it measures everything in short, except that which makes life worthwhile.

Kennedy was assassinated not long after he made that speech, but his vision was indicative of a period of political recognition of need for bold action on the environment. In the hyper-capitalist USA of the 1960s, albeit in a period in which social movements for change were active on a number of fronts, a dazzling number of laws and regulations were passed with the purpose of restraining and redirecting industrial practices that had direct consequences for health and the environment. Here is a partial list:

- The 1964 Federal Trade Commission (FTC) directive requiring health warnings on cigarette labels. In 1971 the FTC banned TV and radio commercials for tobacco.
- The Water Quality Act of 1965 and the more ambitious Water Pollution Control Act of 1972, aiming to restore polluted waterways.
- The Hazardous Substances Labelling Act of 1966 that required warnings on dangerous household products.
- The Child Protection Act of 1966, banning toys and other articles containing hazardous substances.
- The Automobile Safety Act of 1966, requiring automobile manufacturers to install seat belts.
- The Truth in Packaging Act of 1966 requiring content information on products.
- The Air Quality Act of 1967, followed by the more ambitious Clean Air Act of 1970.
- The National Environmental Policy Act of 1970 requiring environmental assessments on federally funded projects.

These laws and regulations put substantial pressure on industry to change their practices and to invest in new technologies; set absolute targets for emissions reductions for sulfur and nitrogen; set energy efficiency standards for the manufacturers of cars and household appliances; and mandated better information for consumers on the energy characteristics of home energy technologies. Many widely used products that were environmentally problematic were banned and for a brief period in the 1970s gasoline was rationed in the USA and European countries. Energy conservation came sharply into focus in the 1970s as a result of the Saudi Arabian oil embargo and President Jimmy Carter's declaration that reducing dependence on energy was the 'moral equivalent of war'. This 'war' was manifested in a wide range of public policies encouraging energy savings and involved stronger public regulating of the energy industry and energy-saving programmes. Many publically owned utilities in the USA and Europe initiated aggressive energy conservation programmes offering low interest loans and subsidies on energy-efficient products to households and commercial businesses. Regulations were passed mandating tougher insulation standards for buildings and more stringent thermal characteristics of windows. Many US cities initiated the construction of collective transport systems or extended existing systems. Automobile manufacturers shifted production to smaller, more fuel-efficient cars, which quickly found a consumer niche. Unfortunately, the focus on small cars and fuel efficiency declined when cheap and abundant gasoline was restored in the 1990s. By 2000, fleet efficiency in the USA had declined to the 1980 level.

This momentum on the environment carried over into the 1980s with the invention of the concept of sustainable development (WCED 1987) and initial enthusiasm about incorporating sustainability into governance from global to local. The publication of *Our Common Future* in 1987 lead to a wave of international interest in sustainable energy and legitimized goal setting and legislation in Europe on climate, energy efficiency and other environmental issues such as biodiversity and waste treatment. Unfortunately, this initial political enthusiasm waned after 1990, despite convincing evidence that human activity was affecting the climate. Concerns for economic growth and industrial competitiveness regained the upper hand over environmental action. This reversal of priorities resulted in the toothless green economy models discussed in Chapter 4 and a decline in the sense of urgency and momentum in government action on energy savings. The growth in climate emissions and in our understanding of the consequences has raced ahead of our capacity to legislate a political economic package of laws and regulations armed to deal with it. If violent climate change is to be avoided the momentum of the early efforts on environment and energy will have to be regained and redoubled. National governments will have to reassert themselves in the formation of laws, regulations and infrastructural changes that aim at a reduction in the numbers of automobiles, sizes of houses, amount of space dedicated to air and food refrigeration and at enabling alternative and less energy-intensive means of travelling, sheltering, heating and cooling buildings and food provisioning and consumption. This will mean government actions and regulations aimed not just at consumers but at producers and providers, including manufacturers, banks, the building industry, energy utilities and media.

Urban initiatives

The UN Rio Earth Summit in 1992 was an attempt to obtain consensus and a commitment from national governments on carbon-reduction targets (as well as other environmental issues) and to encourage the enactment of national policies to reduce energy and carbon. The subsequent record shows that these national efforts have been largely unsuccessful. The Earth Summit also produced Local Agenda 21, a policy vision and action plan for cities and communities that has made an impact on urban environmental initiatives in many parts of the world. Local Agenda 21 was based on an acknowledgement by the summit organizers that efforts to transform environmental impacts at the national level would not be sufficiently rapid or robust to reduce the impact of human activity on the environment and that parallel efforts needed to be encouraged and supported at the local level. While not providing a detailed programme for addressing local action, chapter 28 of Agenda 21 appealed to 'local authorities to engage in a dialogue for sustainable development with the members of their constituencies' (Lafferty 2001: 1). Essentially, the target of Agenda 21 was local political actors, encouraging an opening for the participation of non-governmental groups such as charities, local businesses and labour unions. The goal was to stimulate environmental programmes through the mobilization of new governance alliances between local authorities and representatives of civil society.

According to Guillen-Royo (2015), recent assessments of the effectiveness of Agenda 21 do not credit it with substantial impacts on community planning. Nonetheless, there are indications that in the Nordic countries and several European countries, Agenda 21 has been responsible for a greater emphasis on environmental issues in urban planning and programmes. Lafferty's (2001) review identified cities in the United Kingdom, Denmark, Netherlands, France, Ireland, Austria and Italy that had initiated ambitious environmental planning. Seyfang and Smith (2007) traced the extensive set of city programmes initiated by DEFRA in the United Kingdom to Local Agenda 21. These included 'Community Action 2020', which promoted 'local food initiatives, community energy efficiency schemes, recycling projects and Fairtrade activities, plus participation in decision-making, volunteering, capacity-building, information sharing and community monitoring' (2007: 586). In the USA, the Agenda 21 initiatives merged with an ecological city movement originating in Berkeley, California in 1975 (Roseland 1997). This urban ecology agenda encouraged reduced environmental impact, voluntary simplicity and grassroots participation. It influenced city planning in northern California and cities of the Pacific Northwest, including Portland and Seattle, both of which adopted an 'urban village strategy' in the 1980s, 'which calls for the creation and improvement of walkable communities in which people can walk to jobs, shopping and employment opportunities, and have efficient public access to travel between these villages' (Krueger and Agyeman 2005: 414).

Other city-based initiatives can be traced to energy-saving agendas and climate action. An example of this is the Covenant of Mayors (2015) programme initiated by the European Union. It is careful to define itself as 'a mainstream European movement involving local and regional authorities, voluntarily committing to increasing energy efficiency and use of renewable energy sources on their territories'. The movement emphasizes market incentives and voluntarism as the drivers behind city-based energy initiatives. In Germany, however, several city-based initiatives go beyond market-based environmentalism and aim at reversing the deregulation and commercialization of energy which began in the 1990s, reinstituting public control over energy production and delivery. An example is Hamburg, which in a referendum in 2013 voted to put their electricity, gas and heating grids back under the control of the municipal government (Klein 2014: 97).

In the same year, the city council of Berlin voted to switch from a private to publically owned energy utility. According to Klein, many other municipalities in Germany have since started up public energy utilities.

There are a growing number of cities that are reclaiming urban space from automobiles through infrastructural changes that favour walking and cycling. In some cities, this is complemented by restricting parking and closing off parts of the city to automobiles altogether. Evidence from these urban efforts indicates that despite resistance from automobile associations, transport delivery firms and a few local retail businesses, the restrictions on cars and the reclaiming of urban space for bicycles and walking have been largely viewed as positive by urban inhabitants (Bulkeley et al. 2011). Wallenborn and Wilhite (2014a) review recent developments in urban cycling. There has been a surge in cycling in many European cities because of the building of safe and convenient infrastructure for biking, as well as making it possible to combine public transport with biking (allowing bicycles on trains, buses and ferries). Copenhagen was one of the early cities to build an extensive bicycle infrastructure. Today, 40 percent of commuting within Copenhagen is by bicycle. Stockholm has 750 km of bike paths, and Gothenburg 450 km. Paris has built 600 km of bike paths over the past ten years. San Francisco set a goal of making 10 percent of all trips within the city by bicycle in 2018. The city began building a safe bicycle infrastructure in 2010. A recent evaluation showed that this had led to a 14 percent increase in cycling within in a two-year period and up to 80 percent increases in parts of the city that had installed bike-friendly traffic signals (in addition to bike lanes). An experiment was conducted in San Francisco allowing bicycles on public transport in non-commuting hours. It was so successful that this was extended to all periods of the day. Ten percent of the users of public transportation now travel with bicycles (http://www.sfmta.com/projects-planning/projects/tep-transi t-effectiveness-project). The evidence from San Francisco and many major cities in Europe is that the provision of bicycle infrastructure provides the opportunity for safe experimentation and this sets the stage for a significant increase in cycling.

Enabling practical learning

From a habit perspective, providing practical learning opportunities such as safe bicycle infrastructure is important to engendering change (Lave 1993). As Wallenborn and Wilhite write, experimentation 'can lead to a body-close understanding and demystification of the consequences (for example that biking in Paris is dangerous) and lead to further experimentation with other low-energy practices' (2014a: 61). Practical learning differs dramatically from the usual information highlighting the money-saving potential of energy-saving purchases (Marres 2012). Practical learning emphasizes experimentation with new ways of doing things and learning from peers who have changed their practices. Publically financed demonstration homes such as those established in Davis, California in the 1970s and 1980s are good examples of how policies that enable exposure to new ways of doing things can be a stimulus to reshaping habits.

These demonstration homes were not technology showcases or prototype houses, but rather had real people living in them and interacting with the technologies in the home. Neighbours were invited to observe and experience life in a low-energy house first hand, to talk with the occupants and by doing so, demystify low-energy living. In other words, people responded to observing practices and talking with residents about their experiences, a deeper form for learning than reading information pamphlets or visiting prototype houses without people living in them.

One policy opportunity for influencing within the home habits is when families are in the process of moving from one house to another. Home habits get shaken up because new houses have different material characteristics including size and number of rooms, different heating/cooling systems, different neighbours (if the move is to a new neighbourhood or new city) and different access to roads, public transport, sidewalks and bike paths. As Lahire writes about people in the process of moving from one house to another, 'it seems that the new situation induces them (occupants) to feel that their habits have become strange to them' (2003: 340). Wallenborn and Wilhite (2014a: 63) expand on this point:

> Perceptions are refreshed, material settings change and opportunities for new practices develop. In the new setting, walking or biking may be chosen as a means of commuting to work rather than driving, organic foods given priority over ready-made dishes, or new windows or wall insulation installed, all of which are examples of small experiments that have the taste of mini 'adventures' and expose bodies to new gestures and perceptions. These may reshape the body and can bring new pleasures with less energy.

In other words, household habits get disrupted by these changes, and the period in which households are adapting to their new home is a lucrative period to provide information and incentives on how to reduce energy consumption (Wilk and Wilhite 1985; Lahire 2003; Verplanken and Wood 2006).

Conclusion

This chapter has touched on several of the dilemmas associated with a low carbon transformation. One set of dilemmas could be designated as crises in democracy, first because national political leaders are most interested in shoring up and perpetuating the economic system that measures its success in growth, which then becomes a litmus test for whether or not they will be re-elected. Many of these sincerely believe that making the political economic changes necessary to significantly reduce carbon will cripple the economic system to the extent that there will be massive unemployment and social upheaval. The issue then becomes which is the more potentially devastating of the two scenarios: reconfiguring the political economy to less dependence on energy and carbon, or ignoring the climate change threat and surging ahead with an economic system that will be increasingly environmentally intrusive as the global economy continues to grow.

Given the now quite clear evidence that business as usual, with a few green economy retrofits, will lead to four–six-degree increases in surface temperature, there should no longer be any doubt as to which choice needs to be made.

Another dimension of the democratic crisis is grassroots complacency about the climate crisis, related to the complexities of climate science, the uncertainties about the severity of the consequences and worries about the social and economic consequences of a low carbon society. From which constituency will support for transforming to a low carbon political economy come? As discussed in this chapter, there are positive, yet modest examples of countries that are taking transformation seriously, including Germany with its strong renewable energy goals, Denmark with its long history of efforts to replace fossil fuel with wind energy, and the European Union as a whole is encouraging its member states to set strong energy-efficiency targets. Yet these targets are relative, measuring success by the resulting increase in energy efficiency and not in absolute reductions of energy use. Nowhere in the world is there a national leadership that is aiming to reduce either the size of its economy or making an effort to reduce absolute levels of energy used. There are indications that interest in low carbon transformation is building among young people and in the intentional communities that will be discussed in the next chapter. An interesting development is the involvement of religious organizations and the commitment by Pope Francis to putting climate change on national political agendas. In his first speech to the American people on the White House lawn on 23 September 2015, he named climate change as one of the world's major global challenges. He also brought the message into the US Congress, where religious conservatives who deny the existence of climate change are blocking political action. According to the Guardian (2015), opinion surveys after these speeches, which got wide media coverage, resulted in a 15 percent increase in the number of Americans who are convinced that climate change is happening.

There is a crucial need for climate governance from top to bottom. It will involve a strong political vision that is willing to reassess the relationship between economic prosperity, growth and wellbeing; that reframes the relationship between work, production and consumption; that redirects research funding into projects that generate knowledge on societal transformation and accounts for the ways carbon emissions are generated through the coupling of production, provision, work and consumption. The question remains as to whether and when any national government will acknowledge the need for systemic change in political economy and to take the necessary political action on low carbon transformation. In the next chapter, I will discuss the growing number of communities in which these pillars of capitalism are being addressed and collective efforts being made to transform high energy habits.

References

Appadurai, A. 1986. Introduction: Commodities and the Politics of Value. In A. Appadurai (ed.), *The Social Life of Things: Commodities in a Cultural Perspective*. Cambridge: Cambridge University Press, pp. 3–63.

Bourdieu, Pierre. 1998. *Practical Reason: On the Theory of Action*. Cambridge: Polity.

Bulkeley, H., V. Castán Broto, M. Hodson and S. Marvin (eds). 2011. *Cities and Low Carbon Transitions*. London: Routledge.

Burawoy, Michael. 2011. Theory and Practice: Marx meets Bourdieu. Online essay. Available at http://burawoy.berkeley.edu/Bourdieu/3.Marx.pdf. Accessed 12 December 2014.

Carfagna, L. B., E. A. Dubois, C. Fitzmaurice, M. Y. Ouimette, J. B. Schor, M. Willis and T. Laidley. 2014. An Emerging Eco-Habitus: The Reconfiguration of High Cultural Capital Practices among Ethical Consumers. *Journal of Consumer Culture* 14(2): 158–178.

Carson, Rachel. 1962. *Silent Spring*. Boston, MA: Houghton Mifflin.

Coote, Anna, Jane Franklin and Andrew Simms. 2013. 21 Hours, Key Findings. Report by the New Economics Foundation. Available at: http://www.neweconomics.org/publications/entry/21-hours. Accessed 20 July 2015.

Covenant of Mayors. 2015. Available at http://www.covenantofmayors.eu/index_en.html. Accessed 12 September 2015.

Ehrhardt-Martinez, Karen, Juliet B. Schor, Wokje Abrahamse, Alison Alkon, Jon Axsen, Keith Brown, Rachel Shwom, Dale Southerton and Harold Wilhite. 2015. Consumption and Climate Change. In Riley E. Dunlap and Robert J. Brulle (eds), *Climate Change and Society: Sociological Perspectives*. Oxford: Oxford University Press.

Fine, Ben. 2002. *The World of Consumption: The Material and Cultural Revisited*. London: Routledge.

Foucault, Michel. 1979. *Discipline and Punish: The Birth of the Prison*. Harmondsworth: Penguin.

Guardian. 2015. Rising Numbers of Americans Believe Climate Science, Poll Shows. Available at http://www.theguardian.com/environment/2015/oct/13/rising-numbers-of-american-believe-climate-science-poll-shows. Accessed 18 October 2015.

Guillen-Royo, M. 2015. *Sustainability and Wellbeing: Human Scale Development in Practice*. Abingdon: Routledge.

Hamilton, Clive. 2003. *Growth Fetish*. London: Pluto Press.

Hansen, Arve and Ulrikke Wethal (eds). 2014. *Emerging Economies and Challenges to Sustainability*. London: Routledge.

Hargreaves, T., N. Longhurst and G. Seyfang. 2013. Up, Down and Round: Connecting Regimes and Practices in Innovation for Sustainability. *Environmental Planning A* 45(2): 402–420.

Harvey, David. 2014. *Seventeen Contradictions and the End of Capitalism*. Oxford and New York: Oxford University Press.

Hernandez, Mario. 2012. The Hegemony of Habitus: Locating the Role of Domination and Agency in the Works of Gramsci and Bourdieu. *Interdisciplinary Journal of the New School for Social Research*. Available at http://canononline.org/archives/current-issue-2/the-hegemony-of-habitus-locating-the-role-of-domination-and-agency-in-the-works-of-gramsci-and-bourdieu/. Accessed 28 November 2014.

Hornberg, Alf. 2014. The Fossil Interlude: Euro-American Power and the Return of the Physiocrats. In Sarah Strauss, Stephanie Rupp and Thomas Love (eds), *Cultures of Energy: Power, Practices, Technologies*. Walnut Creek, CA: Left Coast Press, pp. 41–59.

Jackson, Tim 2009. *Prosperity without Growth: Economics for a Finite Planet*. London and Washington, DC: Earthscan.

Klein, Naomi. 2014. *This Changes Everything: Capitalism vs. the Climate*. New York: Simon and Shuster.

Knight, Kyle W., Eugene A. Rosa and Juliet B. Schor. 2013. Could Working Less Reduce Pressures on the Environment? A Cross-National Panel Analysis of OECD Countries, 1970–2007. *Global Environmental Change* 23: 691–700.

Krueger, Rob and Julian Agyeman. 2005. Sustainability Schizophrenia or 'Actually Existing Sustainabilities?': Toward a Broader Understanding of the Politics and Promise of Local Sustainability in the US. *Geoforum* 36: 410–417.

Kurlansky, Mark. 2004. *1968: The Year that Rocked the World*. London:Vintage.

Lafferty, William. 2001. Introduction. In William Lafferty (ed.), *Sustainable Communities in Europe*. London: Earthscan, pp. 1–14.

Lahire, B. 2003. From the Habitus to an Individual Heritage of Dispositions. Towards a Sociology at the Level of the Individual. *Poetics* 38: 329–355.

Lave, Jean. 1993. The Practice of Learning. In S. Chaiklin and J. Lave (eds), *Understanding Practice: Perspectives on Activity and Context*. Cambridge: Cambridge University Press.

Marres, N. 2012. *Material Participation: Technology, the Environment and Everyday Publics*. Basingstoke: Palgrave MacMillan.

McFadden, S. 2012. Unraveling the CSA Number Conundrum. Available at: http://theca llofthe land.wordpress.com/2012/01/09unravaeling-the-csa-number-conundrum/. Accessed 12 September 2015.

McNeill, D. and H. Wilhite. 2015. Making Sense of Sustainable Development in a Changing World. In A. Hansen and U. Wethal (eds), *Emerging Economies and Challenges to Sustainability*. London: Routledge.

Moezzi, M. and L. Lutzenhiser. 2010. What's Missing in Theories of the Residential Energy User. *Proceedings of the 2010 ACEEE Summer Study on Buildings*. Washington, DC: American Council for an Energy Efficient Economy.

Pettersen, I. N. 2015. Fostering Absolute Reductions in Resource Use: The Potential Role and Feasibility of Practice-Oriented Design. *Journal of Cleaner Production*. Available at http://dx.doi.org/10.1016/j.jclepro.2015.02.005. Accessed 17 October 2015.

Polyani, Karl. 1957. *The Great Transformation*. Boston, MA: Beacon Press.

Roseland, Mark. 1997. Dimensions of the Eco-City. *Cities* 14(4): 197–202.

Schor, Juliet. 1992. *The Overworked American: The Unexpected Decline of Leisure*. New York: Basic Books.

Seyfang, Gill. 2009. Low-Carbon Currencies: The Potential of Time Banking and Local Money Systems for Community Carbon-Reduction. CSERGE working paper EDM 09-04. CSERGE, School of Environmental Sciences, University of East Anglia, Cambridge.

Seyfang, Gill and Adrian Smith. 2007. Grassroots Innovations for Sustainable Development: Towards a New Research and Policy Agenda. *Environmental Politics* 16(4): 584–603.

Shove, Elizabeth. 2010. Beyond the ABC: Climate Change Policy and Theories of Social Change. *Environment and Planning* 42: 1273–1285.

Shove, Elizabeth and Gorden Walker. 2010. Governing Transitions in the Sustainability of Everyday Life. *Research Policy* 39(4): 471–476.

Smith, Richard. 2010. Beyond Growth or beyond Capitalism? *Real-World Economics Review* 53: 28–42.

Sovacool, B. K., S. E. Ryan, P. K. Stern, K. Janda, G. Rochlin, D. Spreng, M. J. Pasqualetti, H. Wilhite and L. Lutzenhiser. 2015. Integrating Social Science in Energy Research. *Energy Research and Social Science* 6:95–99.

Tukker, A., M. Cohen, K. Hubacek and O. Mont. 2010. The Impacts of Household Consumption and Options for Change. *Journal of Industrial Ecology* 14(1): 13–30.

Verplanken, Bas and Wendy Wood. 2006. Interventions to Break and Create Consumer Habits. *American Marketing Association* 25(1): 90–103.

Wallenborn, G. and H. Wilhite. 2014a. Rethinking Embodied Knowledge and Household Consumption. *Energy Research and Social Science* 1: 56–64.

Wallenborn, G. and H. Wilhite. 2014b. How Acknowledging the Body Could Inform Policy. Paper presented at the workshop Experts' Round Table on Practice Theory and Complex Adaptive Systems Theory, JRC-IET Ispra, Italy, 26 June.

WCED. 1987. *Our Common Future*. Oxford and New York: Oxford University Press.

Wilhite, H., E. Shove, L. Lutzenhiser and W. Kempton. 2000. The Legacy of Twenty Years of Demand Side Management: We Know More about Individual Behavior but next to Nothing about Demand. In E. Jochem, J. Stathaye and D. Bouille (eds), *Society, Behaviour and Climate Change Mitigation*. Dordrect: Luwer Academic Press.

Wilk, R. and H. Wilhite. 1985. Household Energy Decision Making. In W. Kempton and B. Morrison (eds), *Families and Energy, Coping with Uncertainty*. Lansing, MI: Michigan State University Press.

6 Bottom-up efforts to transform communities, consumption and household habits

There are a growing number of communities worldwide who are changing their community, neighbourhood and household practices in ways that reduce environmental impact. The designation 'intentional community' is sometimes used to describe them because their efforts are purposive and collective. Many of them aim to increase sociality and sharing. Very few of these community movements are explicitly anti-capitalist, but many of them nonetheless either explicitly or implicitly challenge one or more of the pillars of capitalism: economic growth, individual ownership, consumerism and traditional market exchange. Weltzner (2011: 13) writes that these community-centred changes from the bottom up are important from a transformative perspective because, 'The[ir] goal is to devise an exit strategy from growth, not to preserve a cultural practice that undermines our own survival conditions. Such strategies are not the types that can be developed in the usual ill-fated coalitions of "experts" and policymakers. To invent a post-growth society is a project for civil society; its realization cannot be delegated.' In a similar vein, Kallis (2011: 874), based on her research on ecovillages (quoted in Guillen-Royo 2015), writes 'I propose that big social change does not take place by appealing to those in power, but by bottom-up movements that challenge established paradigms'. Krueger and Agyeman (2005: 410), who have studied low-impact communities, point out that they are important because they move the discussion from a debate about utopic visions to an analysis of 'actually existing sustainabilities'.

Pickerill and Maxey (2009) suggest that the diversity and smallness of scale of community actions have been two of the reasons that they have not been drawn into mainstream research on societal transformation. I claim that from a habit perspective these bottom-up, participatory efforts are important sources of information on transformation. They provide examples for researchers, policy makers and householders on how neighbourhoods, communities and networks of people go about changing their habits. They provide information on what sorts of experiments are effective in efforts to adapt to new and less environmentally intrusive practices, including those associated with food, shelter, comfort, transport, cleanliness and entertainment. They are also a source of insights on whether and how these local transformations have the potential to connect, grow and impact on national agendas for low carbon transformation.

I will begin the chapter with a discussion of co-housing, otherwise known as community housing, which is a form of collective, or shared housing that has been catalysed by municipal authorities in a few countries but the main thrust comes from families and individuals seeking to increase social interaction, sharing and spaces for collective living. I will follow this with a discussion of neighbourhood and community transformations which involve not only the sharing of housing, but an effort to make a broad range of community and household practices less environmentally intrusive.

Collaborative housing

The individualizing forces of capitalism have affected ideas and practices about who should live under the same roof. Well into the twentieth century in the USA and Europe it was not uncommon for the house to be regarded as a space to be shared by members of the extended family, including the nuclear family (husband, wife and children), lineal relatives (parents and grandparents) and even aunts, uncles and cousins. During the Great Depression of the 1930s and 1940s, it was not uncommon for families to rent bedrooms to strangers as well as to provide a place for them at the dinner table. Over the course of subsequent generations, the practice of the nuclear family sharing the space of the house with family relatives or renting to strangers has waned, though as I will discuss below, renting rooms or the entire home to vacation renters is a fairly new but rapidly growing practice. In terms of permanent living arrangements, with a few exceptions, such as the case of an elderly parent living in the home, the house is regarded as the domain of the nuclear family and, increasingly in recent decades, the domain of single adults, due to the increasing number of elderly men and women living alone, young people marrying later and to separations and divorces. Looking to Asia and Africa, the joint family household continues to be a fairly common living arrangement, but the nuclear family is emerging in most countries as the modern form of household (Wilhite 2008). As discussed in Chapter 3, house sizes are growing worldwide. Taken together with the reduction in the number of people living in the house, fewer people are sharing larger living spaces. The consequence is an increase in the per person demand for heating and cooling energy as well as an increase in the number of energy-using appliances dedicated to serving the needs of each individual. The expansion of per capita house size and its consequences for energy consumption is a non-issue in national and urban energy-efficiency programmes, where the emphasis has been on 'tight' buildings, 'smart' technologies and energy-efficient appliances (see Chapter 5 for a discussion). Very little has been done from a carbon or energy perspective to encourage the building of smaller houses or the sharing of house space. As the various forms of sharing I will discuss in this chapter demonstrate, sharing has the potential to significantly reduce per capita cooling and heating load as well as the numbers of appliances needed to satisfy household food, cleaning and entertainment practices. I will discuss three types of house sharing: building cooperatives, co-housing and communes.

Building cooperatives consist of a collection of apartments in which the residents have ownership rights to their apartment but who pay a monthly fee to the cooperative that is dedicated to maintenance and services. The cooperative living arrangement usually includes shared spaces, such as laundry rooms, recreation rooms and gardens. Some offer memberships in car-sharing organizations (discussed below) and provide parking for shared cars. Decisions such as those concerning finances, upkeep, renovations and contracts with the energy provider are shared, usually facilitated by an elected governing board. The sense of the collective is also fostered through events such as shared dinners and picnics, as well as informal gatherings in recreation areas and gardens. Scandinavian countries and the Netherlands are the countries in Europe with the highest numbers of building cooperatives, many of them members of umbrella organizations (such as OBOS in Norway) that provide various forms of support and assistance to the individual member cooperatives. OBOS encompasses more than 160,000 row houses and apartment buildings and over 300,000 members, about 200,000 of whom live in the greater Oslo region of Norway (with a population of 900,000). About 25 percent of the population of greater Oslo participates in a form of cooperative housing.

Compared with building cooperatives, in co-shared housing arrangements a greater number of spaces and practices are shared. Co-shared housing encompasses shared living and recreation areas, kitchens, dining rooms, laundry rooms and gardens (Vestbro and Horelli 2012). In many co-shared housing arrangements with common kitchens and dining areas, occupants have their own small kitchen and eating area. This gives occupants the choice as to whether they want to participate in communal meals or prepare and eat their own food privately. Community housing is a variation on co-housing in which participating families have houses that are separate from communal buildings (Seyfang and Smith 2007; Lietaert 2010). Individual families live in their own compact house (most often a row house) but have access to communal kitchens, dining areas, recreation rooms and clothes-washing facilities. According to Seyfang and Smith who reviewed and analysed community housing projects in the United Kingdom, in a typical community 'The common house contains a large kitchen and dining area for shared meals, and industrial-sized washing machines and lawn mowers. Cars are kept to the perimeter (and may be shared), allowing for open gardens and footpaths between houses' (2007: 588). The goal is a 'creative mix' of private and common dwellings designed to create a sense of community while preserving a high degree of individual privacy.

The majority of these co-housing and community housing projects involve participatory decision making and many make participation in shared activities such as maintenance, repairs, food preparation and child care mandatory. Lietaert (2010: 578) assessed co-housing projects in Europe and concluded that their success is dependent on the active participation of the residents in governance and shared activities. Lietaert found that new 'habits' had formed in these cooperatives involving a greater degree of sharing of both goods and services. He writes that

Cohousers above all create sharing systems of small items such as tools for gardening, maintenance, cleaning tools, cooking, small furniture, camping, etc. They also often share clothes for babies and children. And they are pretty well organized for sharing medium sized devices such as freezers, washing machines, lawn mowers, etc. The daily use of cars is also diminished for example, as use of bicycles and car-sharing grows.

Lietaert (2010) suggests that the retention of separate incomes (rather than pooling incomes) and spaces set aside for the private use of each participant (or participating family) are important to the success of co-housing. He is sceptical as to the co-housing models that are organized communes, in which participants pool incomes and in which they have little or no private space. The commune as household form had a hiatus in Europe and the USA in the 1960s and 1970s, attracting mainly young people who rejected what they regarded as their parents' materialistic lifestyles and combined shared living with anti-consumerism and participation in civil movements and protests (see Norman Mailer's 1968 *Armies of the Night*). By the 1980s most of these communes had dissolved and their participants were reintegrating into conventional forms of housing and work. Communal living is now mainly regarded as a transitional phase that a few university students and other young people pass through on the way to conventional jobs, families and solid incomes. The commune as housing concept has waned but the interest in sharing, recreating community and de-emphasizing the importance of material consumption is growing and spreading in many parts of the world.

Reshaping community

There are many localized efforts around the world in which the aims are much broader than co-housing. These are communities in which participants aim to share food provisioning and consumption; encourage community-based enterprises; increase non-market and other forms of exchange; and take other measures to reduce the community's energy use and environmental footprint, such as reducing energy consumption, recycling and composting. In other words, while differing substantially in motives, these communities either directly or indirectly challenge the pillars of capitalist political economy, as well as aiming at breaking and reforming household habits. Some of these are 'intentional communities' based on religious beliefs, while others are motivated by a desire for simple living and material 'downshifting'. Examples of intentional communities are the Amish and Mennonite communities in the USA, as well as a few secular communities in New England and California with their roots in the counter-culture movement of the 1960s. These usually locate themselves in rural areas, and as Stable (2000) writes, have a 'retreat mentality', with little or no interest influencing mainstream ways of living. Reducing energy use and environmental impact are not necessarily explicit goals for many of these communities, but rather a consequence of their low material lifestyles. Concerning community transformations with an explicit environmental motive, the transition movement and ecovillage are two of the largest and fastest growing. Both of these were initiated from below by groups of people operating outside of, or living and working against the grain of conventional political structures and processes. They are characterized by bottom-up, participatory efforts to comprehensively reshape production and consumption in ways that reduce environmental impacts. Both of them involve networks of communities and towns that share experiences, thus promoting community-to-community and peer-to-peer learning.

The transition movement began in the United Kingdom in 2005 in the city of Totnes, which designated itself as a 'transition town' and set about reducing its environmental footprint through a participatory process. The transition town concept spread to other cities in the UK and grew into the transition movement. The movement has since expanded to many other European countries and to other parts of the world, such as Canada, the USA and Australia. As of 2014, more than 1,100 towns had joined the transition network (Salvesen 2014). In order to be eligible to join the movement, a community must commit to certain principles, including participatory planning and an aim to be less environmentally intrusive. According to Hopkins (2007), the transition movement is based on a vision that is not anti-capitalist but rather 'non-capitalist', because of its principles of collaboration, sharing and low-impact living. Transition towns put emphasis on community and collectivity in both decision making and in material and housing arrangements. They incorporate a positive vision of life quality rather than one of denial or simplicity. An interesting finding from Salvesen's (2014) study of the nascent transition movement in Norway is that many participants do not identify themselves as 'environmentalists'. Participants are interested in reducing the energy use and climate impact of their everyday lives and many are sceptical of weak national political efforts to resolve the climate crisis, but most emphasize that their main motive in joining is the desire to strengthen community. As one member of the transition movement in the Norwegian community of Landås put it, the environmental gains were a 'nice bonus' that came on top of strengthening community ties and interactions (Salvesen 2014: 79).

The transition experience in Totnes is now ten years in the making and provides an interesting empirical case for analysing the community transformative process. Totnes began with changing food production and consumption practices, emphasizing the creation of famers markets, aggregating demand for products from local growers and setting up local gardening projects in which people could benefit not only from a diet centred on organic food, but could also derive health benefits from using their bodies to plant food, maintain gardens and harvest the products. More recently Totnes has taken actions to reduce the community's energy consumption. In 2010, Totnes initiated the Transition Streets Project, aimed at lowering energy use by changing consumption practices related to home energy use, transportation, food and waste. The way they went about this drew on the principles of practical learning (discussed in Chapter 5). Householders were encouraged to find five or six other households willing to participate. The group then attended a workshop with a transition facilitator, were given a workbook and encouraged to meet at each other's houses once or twice a week. More than 500 households participated in the programme. An evaluation of the results showed that the project resulted in a reduction of carbon emissions of 1.3 tonnes and a reduction in household energy bills of £570 (Guillen-Royo 2015). The Totnes community has also set up experiments in practical learning with outsiders, inviting outside participants to workshops with community members and organizing interactive walks through the town once a week (http://www.transitiontowntotnes.org). This approach to change utilizing demonstrations, experimentation and peer learning is a good example of the approach needed to break and reform habits. These transition movement experiences deserve greater attention in low carbon research.

The ecovillage is another global community-based movement emphasizing collaboration, community and low environmental impact. According to Lifkin (2014), the roots of the ecovillage draw on the writings of Aldo Leopold, and his book published in 1949, *A Sand Country Almanac*. He put forward the idea that nature and land should be regarded as endogenous to community and that the commodification and privatization of nature in the West had degraded both community life and ecological health. This integrated community-ecology concept informed permaculture movements in many parts of the world, in which an effort was made to reintegrate nature and natural processes into both agricultural practices and village life in rural communities. Ecovillages in different regions of the world have drawn on community and ecology movements particular to the region. In the USA and Europe, the ecovillage has drawn on the social movements of the 1970s and the co-housing and 'back-to-the-land' movements of the 1990s. Lifkin (2014) writes that in Asia, the ideas of Gandhian self-sufficiency and spirituality were important to ecovillage formation. In Latin America, the ecovillage drew on the participatory development and alternative technology movements.

In some parts of Europe and the USA, the ecovillage has been incorporated into larger communities where, as anthropologist Tim Ingold (2000) suggests, many people feel that the natural world is absent in their everyday lives. As Bang (2005, quoted in Kasper 2008: 13) summarizes the ecovillage concept, 'the goal (of the ecovillage) is the harmless integration of human activities into the environment in a way that supports healthy human development in physical, emotional, mental, and spiritual ways, and is able to continue into the indefinite future'. The ecovillage concept is more explicitly environmental in its goals than the transition movement and more radical in its challenge to conventional political economy. It combines the goals of minimal environmental intrusion, social inclusion and collective decision making. It challenges the capitalist fundaments of private ownership and individual accumulation. The number of communities subscribing to the ecovillage concept had grown sufficiently by the 1990s to draw support from Local Agenda 21 and for proponents to gather at a conference in Findhorn, Scotland in 1995. The Global Ecovillage Network (GEN) was formed and shortly thereafter recognized by the United Nations Economic and Social Council. By 2008 there were 347 ecovillages officially registered with GEN, but this is only a fraction of the total estimated by Jackson a few years earlier, Jackson (2004) estimated this was only a fraction of the to be approximately 15,000 ecovillages worldwide (Jackson 2004).

Anthropologist Debbie Kasper (2008) studied the ecovillage concept and the ways it is put into practice in eight ecovillages in the USA. Based on her ethnographic study, she found that while the eight villages had somewhat different approaches and models for community life, their overall aims were to regenerate the social and environmental fabrics of life, putting strong emphasis on community and participation. Similar to the findings of Salvesen on the motives of members of the transition movement, Kasper found that the majority of the ecovillage participants she studied did not see themselves 'as particularly environmentally-minded'; rather, strengthening community came first. As one of the ecovillage residents formulated her motive for joining, it was 'a longing for community, a safer environment, and a good atmosphere for children' (2008: 14).

From the perspective of changing habits, an interesting finding from Kasper's study is the ecovillage emphasis on the embodiment of new practices. 'The ecovillage paradigm is not only different from the dominant western world-view, it is an understanding of the world that is consciously articulated *and* embodied in ecovillage practices, relations, and the physical setting itself' (2008: 23). The ecovillagers studied by Kasper conveyed an 'acute awareness' of the 'practical importance...and the ecological implications of daily processes like eating, bathing, and disposing of waste' (2008: 18). The sharing of goods, work and entertainment is important in all of these domains of ecovillage life. Many ecovillages deploy the co-housing principles discussed above, building a combination of shared and private spaces. Common to all of the ecovillages studied by Kasper were shared facilities for meals, laundry, recreation and meetings. The buildings and houses in the community were constructed with a view to minimizing both space and energy use. 'A priority in all of these communities is the minimization of spaces that are limited in functionality and that require high energy inputs to construct and maintain' (2008: 17). There is evidence that these ecovillage practices of sharing, reusing, recycling and compact living spaces have had a positive environmental impact. In Lifkin's (2014) study of 14 ecovillages from a number of geographical settings including the USA, Europe, Asia and Africa, she estimated that the community ecological footprints were from 10 to 50 percent smaller than the national average.

Another of Kasper's important findings is that the participants do not intend their communities to be regarded either as utopias or as requiring sacrifice from their members. The ecovillage members she interacted with 'expressed a desire to demonstrate to others the genuine possibility of an alternative lifestyle' (2008: 19). Participants want their community to appeal to 'mainstream Americans' and to project an image of abundance rather than poverty. Similar to the Totnes community practices, ecovillages sponsor classes, workshops and apprenticeships for outsiders. One of the ecovillagers cited by Kasper emphasized the importance of experimentation and practical learning when she said 'information is not the place to start...the problems stem from a deeper source – how they [people] experience themselves in the world'. Kasper captured this emphasis on learning through lived experience in the following way: 'By creating a certain way of experiencing the world, in addition to promoting an intellectual understanding of the reasons for living this way, ecovillages represent the synthesis of knowledge and action, theory and practice...the reformation of deep-seated habits, standards, and preferences, in relevant ways takes time and ongoing effort' (2008: 20). This is a clearly formulated mandate for what is needed to break the habits of capitalism and refashion low carbon political economies on a larger societal scale.

While ecovillages see themselves as important examples of positive change from a social and environmental perspective, they are not actively political or revolutionary in their aims. There are a few alternative community movements in Latin America that explicitly aim to challenge national political economy (Mexico's Zapatistas, for example; see Mattei and Nader 2008), but in the period after the 1970s such challenges are few and far between in the rich countries of the world. One exception is the Low Impact Development (LID) movement in Great Britain that began in the 1990s. It has many similar goals to the ecovillage and transition programmes (such as urban allotments for gardening, city farms, ecobuildings, carpooling, wind energy generation and collective composting and recycling), but LID has also made it clear that its political agenda is anti-capitalist and that it sees itself as an experiment in forging alternatives. Pickerill and Maxey (2009: 1518) write that LID is 'a radical approach to housing, livelihoods and everyday living'. LID is not a 'disconnected idyll' but a 'direct response to the needs for social housing, an anti-capitalist strategy forging alternative economic possibilities, and a holistic approach to living that pays attention to the personal as well as the political'. Pickerill and Maxey contend that LID has 'developed and contributed to the evolution of sustainable technologies and agricultural practices' in Great Britain, but if they are to have a greater impact their accomplishments need to be 'networked and actively promoted at regional and national scales' (2009: 1534).

Could these community experiences serve as a model for a larger scale transformation? When stretched beyond the level of neighbourhood or village, the ability to maintain the sense of community so important to the success of the transformation is a challenge. In the USA there are a few examples of major cities that are deploying the principles of urban ecovillages (Los Angeles, Cleveland and Detroit) but these examples are still few and far between. The efforts in Ecuador and Bolivia to incorporate ecological and communal principles into their national constitutions are noteworthy examples of national efforts that can serve as examples for other countries. In at least one country in Europe, Great Britain, the experiences of the transition movement has apparently influenced the policies of the Department of Environment, Food and Rural Affairs' 'Community Action 2020', which promotes 'local food initiatives, community energy efficiency schemes, recycling projects and Fairtrade activities, as well as participation in decision-making, volunteering, capacity-building, information – sharing and community-mentoring' (Seyfang and Smith 2007: 586). These transformation-oriented communities and their networks are spreading rapidly and many of them are showing interest in sharing information and experiences. Conventional political institutions are paying more attention to them, both because they are a source of knowledge on sustainable living and because of a demand by a growing number of communities and community politicians for sources of inspiration for greening their communities and improving the commons (Crossley 2002). There is a growing research interest in this question of whether community-based movements have the potential to challenge national political structures and influence broader sustainability agendas (Crossley 2002, Seyfang and Smith 2007, Christakis and Fowler 2009, North 2011, Hardt 2013, Geels 2014, Salvesen 2014). This research questions whether and how these community 'niches' in which 'networks of actors experiment with, and mutually adapt, greener organizational forms and eco-friendly technologies' can impact on national sustainability agendas (Seyfang and Smith 2007: 598). This research and the communities themselves deserve greater attention and support from low carbon programmes and policy initiatives.

Collaborative consumption

The examples discussed thus far of collaborative efforts to strengthen community and foster environmentally sustainable practices involve geographically localized participants. Many forms of non-localized collaboration are also growing in housing and transportation, emphasizing reuse, recycling and sharing. Collaborators might be spread across cities, nations or the globe and their interaction facilitated by the internet. Collaborations may be organized in the form of non-profit organizations, cooperatives or commercial businesses. Botsman and Rogers (2010) review these emerging forms of collaborative consumption and sharing. They write that these are eclectic and include such diverse collaborative practices as 'swap trading, time banks, local exchange trading systems (LETS), bartering, social lending, peer-to-peer currencies, tool exchanges, land share, clothing swaps, toy sharing, shared workspaces, co-housing, co-working, CouchSurfing, car sharing, crowdfunding, bike sharing, ride sharing, food co-ops, walking school buses, shared microcreche, peer-to-peer rental' (2010: 71). Many of these collaborations have their roots in the pre-internet era, such as car sharing, carpooling, flea markets, used book outlets, equipment renting, child care and the lending, renting and sharing of vacation property. The internet is facilitating these collaborations and providing a medium for new collaborations. As Ehrhardt-Martinez et al. (2015) point out, non-co-located sharing initiatives have been enhanced by developments in internet software, which saves time and addresses problems of trust between strangers.

The motives of collaborative consumers are sometimes overtly environmental, but economic and practical concerns are also important, such as avoiding the costs and hassles of owning an automobile or avoiding the costs of new clothing for children as they age and grow. Regardless of motive, these collaborations are interesting from a habits-of-capitalism perspective, because many of them de-emphasize the importance of individual ownership, encourage product longevity and reuse, and establish new routines for transport, clothing and housing that are less material- and energy intensive. 'Sharing is believed to reduce climate impacts because it reduces the demand for energy and durable goods (e.g. sharing cars, rides or tools); reduces the need for buildings (e.g. peer-to-peer lodging sites reduce hotel demand); or recirculates goods and materials (e.g. reuse of construction material; clothing; toys, book, and other goods swapping or resale)' (Ehrhardt-Martinez et al. 2015: 115).

Car sharing is an example of a rapidly growing collaborative practice that takes on a deeply entrenched set of everyday transport habits related to the ownership and use of automobiles. Participants forfeit the freedom and flexibility of having their own car, opting instead for shared access to a fleet of cars parked in convenient, nearby locations which can be reserved, used and billed through an internet-based system. Car-sharing members pay a flat membership fee and for the number of kilometres driven, avoiding costs of depreciation, insurance, maintenance and parking. Most car-sharing organizations offer a number of different types of cars (vans, sedans, sports cars) so that the car selected can be suited to the activity, whether it be shopping, transporting heavier goods or visiting friends and relatives. Some of the larger car-share organizations are based on cooperative principles, such as Mobility Switzerland and StattAuto in Germany. Others are commercially organized, such as Zip Car in the USA.

A study by Attali and Wilhite (2001) of car-sharing organizations in Europe and North America found that new members regarded the practical trade-offs associated with forfeiting car ownership were less difficult to deal with than the breaking of the deep-seated notion that owning a car is 'normal'. This was brought home to the participants in the Norwegian car-sharing collective by the persistent questions of neighbours, family and colleagues about why the family had forfeited their car (Wilhite 1997). Despite these social pressures, the results of a survey of the Norwegian participants showed that most participants found that the benefits of car sharing outweighed the burdens of owning a car. This is consistent with studies of car-sharing organizations in many parts of the world which conclude that participants are satisfied with the trade-off between the freedom to have a car parked in their garage and accessible on a moment's notice, with the flexibility of having access to a number of different kinds of cars while avoiding of parking hassles, car maintenance and insurance costs (Attali and Wilhite 2001). A well-functioning, practical system for accessing cars and paying for the use of the car was found to be crucial to success. This includes the provision of ample parking sites for shared vehicles, efficient and reasonable car ordering and payment systems and good management of peak demand for cars. The internet has played a crucial role in making car sharing convenient and practical, making online ordering of cars and online payments possible.

The number of car-sharing members worldwide grew from 350,000 in 2006 to 5 million in 2014, and the number of cars shared from 100,000 to 1 million (Levine et al. 2014). Most of the growth is in Europe and North America, but new organizations are springing up in Latin America and Asia. Other forms of sharing privately owned cars for single journeys, such as the internet-based system commercialized by Uber, are also growing rapidly worldwide, but the use of these is mainly as a supplement to car ownership, rather than a replacement for the car. Car sharing involves a new set of transport practices in which the car plays a much less significant role. From an energy-saving perspective, Attali and Wilhite (2001) found that membership in a car-sharing organization consistently leads to a 40 to 50 percent reduction in kilometres driven. The study pointed to other benefits from a low carbon perspective including the reduced energy needed to produce and dispose of fewer cars.

Home sharing has exploded in the last decade with the establishment of internet-based organizations such as Airbnb, Couchsurfing and HomeExchange. The growth of the largest of these, Airbnb, attests to the rapid increase in home sharing in just a few years. The company was founded in 2008 and by 2011 it had registered its millionth booking. Airbnb bookings continued to increase to 5 million in 2012 and 9 million in 2013. In order to participate, home owners list their homes (or spaces in the home) on the internet sites provided by these companies. Potential renters browse the sites, keeping an eye out for the house, price and location that suit their tastes and travel plans. Staying in homes has certain advantages over hotel rooms, including access to kitchens, washing machines, tumble dryers and playrooms for children, as well as multiple bedrooms. Huber (unpublished manuscript) has examined house sharing in Germany and found that more than 20 percent of the German population have booked rooms in private homes, and over 50 percent of Germans in the age group 30–9.

Sharing and collaboration are also growing in food production and consumption, both of which have important environmental and energy consequences. In the countries of the south, the primary motivation for urban agriculture initiatives has been to increase capacity for food production to supply food to growing urban populations (Mougeot 2011; Sage 2015). Urban agriculture in developing countries is being supported through international development programmes, local city governments and non-government organizations. In the rich Organisation for Economic Co-operation and Development (OECD) countries, the urban garden initiatives have mainly been associated with broader urban greening initiatives, some of which have been supported by city governments, but in the cities where these have flourished, such as Tokyo, London, Portland, Seattle and New Orleans, there have been important contributions from grassroots collaborations, or 'citizens movements'. Many of these offer classes and workshops on urban gardening in which local farmers participate. In Tokyo and other large Japanese cities, demand for space for urban gardens has been so great that there is not enough public space available to accommodate the demand. The demand for gardening space in Tokyo is estimated to be three times the space available (Moreno-Penaranda 2011). These urban food initiatives are important from a low carbon perspective because they actively involve people in the production of their own food, encourage a greater portion of vegetables in dietary choices, reduce the demand for energy-intensive agricultural production and reduce the energy needed to transport commercial agricultural products from farm to consumer.

Conclusion

From a low carbon perspective, there are two good reasons for identifying and paying attention to these developments in community and collaborative consumption. The first is that they provide rich empirical examples of how everyday habits grounded in growth, individual ownership and market environmentalism are being softened and reformed. As Seyfang and Smith (2007: 594) put it, 'A world within a world, grassroots innovations are a demonstration that another way is possible, building alternative infrastructures to the existing regime'. One of the most interesting findings from studies of transition and ecovillage communities, as well as from collaborations in co-housing and car sharing, is that social and practical advantages weigh as importantly as environmental amelioration for many and perhaps most participants. These are not just experiments in sustainable living, but in collaborative social economics in which a healthy environment is only one of several goals among others that include improvements in sociality, convenience and practical advantages such as sharing healthy food production and consumption, avoiding hassles of ownership, reducing energy costs and establishing convenient recycling and reuse. While the motivation for the majority of these communities has not been to overtly challenge capitalism, the emphasis on sharing and scaling down the size of individual living spaces, and extending product life through the sharing and circulation of goods, challenge the fundamental imperatives of capitalism to increase the tempo of consumption and to grow the economy.

The second reason that these community and collaborative developments are interesting from a low carbon perspective is their potential to grow, interconnect and eventually influence practices on a larger scale. As Klein points out, every major socio-political change in US history, from the abolition of slavery, to the response to the Great Depression, to the civil rights movement in the 1960s were successful because 'the project of changing society was deeply woven into the projects of life. Activists were, quite simply, everyone' (2014: 459). These collaborative initiatives must contend with capitalism's drive to undermine collective social and economic relations (Krueger and Agyeman 2005). An important question for future research is the extent to which these community and collaborative transformative efforts, which are so far limited to small groups of people who are committed to change, have the potential to expand in scale to encompass larger numbers of people and higher levels of political organization.

Many scholars are sceptical of this potential for scaling up, arguing that habituation to ownership and control of space and things is so deeply embedded in modern life that an erosion of these habits is unlikely on a wider scale. Salleh (2012: 143) looks to the countries of the south as more likely to absorb these collaborative, local efforts into national political economies. She writes that

'Significantly, the only Major Groups demanding fundamental material changes in the global economy are people involved in the hands-on regeneration of natural processes: women want their reproductive labor contributions valued; peasant farmers want community food sovereignty prioritized; and Indigenous peoples want secure land and biodiversity rights'. In parts of Africa, as well as places like India, China and Brazil, which are rapidly integrating into global capitalism while individualizing processes are taking place, there remain strong traditions of sharing and collaboration (Wilhite 2008). In Africa, an increasing number of scholars associate a return to collective economic and social organization with a revitalization of traditional African social organization and 'decolonization', which Mignolo defines as 'moving toward and building psychologies and subjectivities consistent with communal and pluriversal futures' (2011: 36). An example is a revival of South Africa of interest in *Ubuntu*, named frequently by Nelson Mandela in his strategy for reconciliation and unification. *Ubuntu* stresses the importance of community, solidarity, caring and sharing and emphasizes that human potential can only be realized in partnership with others (Ngcoya 2009; Gade 2012).

Sennett (2012), in his call for a renewal of cooperation in economic and social life, makes the point that in Europe and North America, collective and cooperative economies were common prior to the Industrial Revolution. He writes that 'people's capacities for cooperation are far greater and more complex than institutions allow them to be...Cooperation is embedded in our genes, but cannot remain stuck in routine behavior; it needs to be developed and deepened' (2012: 280). Community movements discussed in this chapter are living examples of how collections of people are practising cooperative economies and reshaping their everyday habits. They deserve greater attention in efforts to break and reform the habits of capitalism.

References

Attali, Sophie and Harold Wilhite. 2001. Assessing Variables Supporting and Impeding the Development of Car Sharing. Proceedings of the ECEEE 2001 Summer Study. Paris: European Council for an Energy Efficient Economy.

Bang, J. M. 2005. *Ecovillages: A Practical Guide to Sustainable Communities*. Gabriola Island, Canada: New Society Publishers.

Botsman, Rachel and Roo Rogers. 2010. *What's Mine Is Yours: How Collaborative Consumption Is Changing the Way We Live*. London: Collins.

Christakis, Nicholas A. and James H. Fowler. 2009. *Connected: The Surprising Power of Our Social Networks and How They Shape Our Lives*. New York: Little, Brown and Company.

Crossley, Nick. 2002. *Making Sense of Social Movements*. Buckingham: Open University Press.

Ehrhardt-Martinez, Karen, Juliet B. Schor, Wokje Abrahamse, Alison Alkon, Jon Axsen, Keith Brown, Rachel Shwom, Dale Southerton and Harold Wilhite. 2015. Consumption and Climate Change. In Riley E. Dunlap and Robert J. Brulle (eds), *Climate Change and Society: Sociological Perspectives*. Oxford: Oxford University Press.

Gade, C. 2012. What Is Ubuntu? Different Interpretations among South Africans of African Descent. *South African Journal of Philosophy* 31(3): 484–503.

Geels, Frank W. 2014. Regime Resistance against Low-Carbon Transitions: Introducing Politics and Power into the Multi-Level Perspective. *Theory, Culture and Society* 31(5): 21–40.

Guillen-Royo, M. 2015. *Sustainability and Wellbeing: Human Scale Development in Practice*. Abingdon: Routledge.

Hardt, E. 2013. In Transition: The Politics of Place-Based Prefigurative Social Movements. MBA dissertation, University of Massachusetts-Amherst. Paper 174.

Hopkins, R. 2007. The Transition Towns Concept. Paper presented at the conference One Planet Agriculture: Preparing for a Post-Peak Oil Food and Farming Future, 25 January, Bristol.

Huber, Andreas. Unpublished manuscript. In press. Theorising the Dynamics of Collaborative Consumption Practices: A Comparison of Peer-to-Peer Accommodation and Cohousing.

Ingold, Tim. 2000. *The Perception of the Environment: Essays in Livelihood, Dwelling, and Skill*. London: Routledge.

Jackson, R. 2004. The Ecovillage Movement. *Permaculture Magazine* 40: 25–30.

Kallis, Georgos. 2011. In Defence of Degrowth. *Ecological Economics* 70: 873–880.

Kasper, Debbie Van Schyndel. 2008. Redefining Community in the Ecovillage. *Human Ecology Review* 15(1): 12–24.

Klein, Naomi. 2014. *This Changes Everything: Capitalism vs. the Climate*. New York: Simon and Shuster.

Krueger, Rob and Julian Agyeman. 2005. Sustainability Schizophrenia or 'Actually Existing Sustainabilities?': Toward a Broader Understanding of the Politics and Promise of Local Sustainability in the US. *Geoforum* 36: 410–417.

Leopold, Aldo. 1949. *A Sand County Almanac: And Sketches Here and There*. Oxford: Oxford University Press.

Levine, Scott, Alereza Zolfaghari and John Polak. 2014. *Car Sharing: Evolution, Challenges and Opportunities*. London: Centre for Transport Studies, Imperial College.

Lietaert, Matthieu. 2010. Cohousing's Relevance to Degrowth Theories. *Journal of Cleaner Production* 18: 576–580.

Lifkin, Karen T. 2014. *Eco-Villages: Lessons for Sustainable Community*. Cambridge: Polity Press.

Mailer, Norman. 1968. *Armies of the Night: History as a Novel: The Novel as History*. New York: New American Library.

Mattei, Uggo and Laura Nader. 2008. *Plunder: When the Rule of Law Is Illegal*. London: Blackwell.

Mignolo, Walter D. 2011. *The Darker Side of Western Modernity: Global Futures, Decolonial Options*. Durham, NC and London: Duke University Press.

Moreno-Penaranda, Raquel. 2011. Japan's Urban Agriculture: Cultivating Sustainability and Well-being. United Nations University publication 2011–19/20.

Mougeot, Luc J. A. 2011. International Support to Research and Policy on Urban Agriculture (1996–2010): Achievements and Challenges. *Urban Agriculture Magazine* 25: 12–17.

Ngcoya, Mvuselelo. 2009. *Ubuntu: Globalization, Accommodation, and Contestation in South Africa*. Ann Arbor, MI: ProQuest LLC.

North, P. 2011. The Politics of Climate Activism in the UK: A Social Movement Analysis. *Environment and Planning* 43: 1581–1598.

Pickerill, Jenny and Maxey Marsh. 2009. Low Impact Development: The Future in Our Hands. Published under the Creative Commons Attribution-Non-Commercial-Share Alike 3.0 licence. Available at http://creativecommons.org/licenses/by-nc-sa/3.0/. Accessed 6 June 2015.

Sage, Colin. 2015. The Transition Movement and Food Sovereignty: From Local Resilience to Global Engagement in Food System Transformation. *Journal of Consumer Culture* 14(2): 254–275.

Salleh, Ariel. 2012. Green Economy or Green Utopia? Rio+20 and the Reproductive Labor Class. *American Sociological Association* 18(2): 141–145.

Salvesen, Ingerid. 2014. Practicing or Preaching? A Study of the Transition Movement in Norway and Its Effort to Change Energy-Related Practices. Master's thesis, Centre for Development and the Environment, University of Oslo.

Sennett, Richard. 2012. *Together: The Rituals, Pleasures and Politics of Cooperation.* New Haven, CT and London: Yale University Press.

Seyfang, Gill and Adrian Smith. 2007. Grassroots Innovations for Sustainable Development: Towards a New Research and Policy Agenda. *Environmental Politics* 16(4): 584–603.

Stable, Donald. 2000. *Community Associations: The Emergence and Acceptance of a Quiet Innovation in Housing.* Westport, CT: Greenwood Press.

Vestbro, D. U. and L. Horelli. 2012. Design for Gender Equality: The History of Co-housing Ideas and Realities. *Built Environment* 38: 315–335.

Weltzner, Harald. 2011. Mental Infrastructures: How Growth Entered the World and Our Souls. Berlin: Heinrich-Boll-Stiftung.

Wilhite, Harold. 1997. *En kvalitativ analyse av motiver, holdninger og bruksmønstre hos medlemmer i bilkollektivet i Oslo.* Oslo: Ressurskonsult A/S.

Wilhite, H. 2008. *Consumption and the Transformation of Everyday Life: A View from South India.* Basingstoke and New York: Palgrave Macmillan.

7   Conclusion

Books like this that argue for deep changes in the conduct of our social and economic lives are usually met with accusations that they suffer from a lack of realism. There is an unwillingness to risk threatening socio-economic systems that deliver jobs, welfare and prosperity for some of us. These are relevant concerns, but in the case of climate change they deny or avoid the stark ecological reality that not only threatens the continuation of economy and prosperity as we know it, but also threatens to alter the global ecology in irreversible and potentially destructive ways. Which reality should take precedence, a troubled economic system making social and economic promises it is not capable of delivering, or an ecosystem in danger of entering a phase of traumatic consequences for life on this planet, both human and non-human? In the rich countries of the world, our political leadership, key economic agents and the vast majority of the rest of us have denied the urgency of climate change for a half century, partly due to the political-economic inertia grounded in deeply anchored political practices encouraging growth in material consumption, but also because the logic of capitalism is rooted in habits formed around central activities in everyday lives. The stark realities of climate change make this habitus of capitalism untenable. It is long past time for those of us in the rich countries of the world, habituated to expansive individualized living spaces and transport devices, beef-intensive food practices, energy-generated thermal comfort and commodity-dense cleaning and cosmetic practices, to accept their ecological consequences and to make the necessary low impact transformations in the ways we frame political economy and live out our everyday lives. To reiterate the central message of this book: the politics of low carbon will require a reinvention of political economy that puts prosperity before growth and that aims at breaking and reforming high energy habits.

The task of reshaping habits will be formidable. The habitus of capitalism encompasses 'the marketing society, the sovereignty of the consumer and all of the anthropocentrism, individualism, materialism and celebration of competition implied by it' (Hamilton 2003: 134). As van Geithuysen (2010: 593) puts it, 'By entering the competitive race to future profit (which they are forced to do in order to avoid economic elimination) economic agents condemn themselves to adopt the particular economic rationality of capitalism, where ecological and social considerations are subordinated to the quest of increasing property value'. In its relationship to nature, capitalism has lived on 'extractivism...a nonreciprocal, dominance based relationship with the earth', and, in the words of Klein (2014: 169), has engendered 'a habit of thought that goes a long way toward explaining why an economic model based on endless growth ever seemed viable in the first place'. As Altvater argues, 'Capitalism was the most dynamic social system in the history of mankind because of the congruence of social forms and mechanisms, rationality and energy provision. A society based on renewable instead of fossil energy sources must develop adequate technologies and above all social forms beyond capitalism' (2007: 59).

As long as the global economy was characterized by a very small part of humanity being served by a plentiful global reservoir of raw materials and cheap labour, capitalism was successful in fostering rapid development to previously unthinkable levels of material affluence. The fact that capitalism worked well under what Weltzner refers to as these 'old conditions' – 'the availability of an entire planet for a small part of humanity and its economic model' – contribute to the difficulties in accepting the need for change (2011: 33). In the words of Mitchell (2011: 215), capitalism has thrived on a 'de-natured politics', made possible by Weltzner's old conditions. The 'new conditions' include a growing global population being increasingly absorbed into the global capitalist system and the now undeniable evidence that CO_2 emissions are accumulating in the troposphere and changing the climate. These new conditions require an acknowledgement that the global ecosystem cannot continue to support a growing global economy and the 'de-naturing' of politics.

Denial and resistance to transforming habits

Many of the agents and institutions that have benefited economically and politically from the 'old conditions' on which capitalist political economies have thrived are actively resisting the deep changes needed to reduce carbon emissions. From a reading of Chapter 6, we see that many local communities around the world have understood and accepted the need for transformation and are at various stages of making it happen. At the scale of nation, region and globe, transformative processes are still being hindered by denial and resistance, coupled in some cases with an active destabilization of political efforts to initiate a low carbon transformation. This denial takes two general forms: one is a denial that climate change and other ecological problems are serious; another acknowledges the seriousness of climate change and its consequences, but takes a position, often accompanied by a large dose of self-interest, that a change of political economic system towards contraction and cooperation will bring with it more problems than it will resolve.

Climate change 'denialists' can be found in virtually every Organisation for Economic Co-operation and Development (OECD) country but climate denial has dwindled as a political force in the European Union, where governments began paying serious attention to climate science in the 1980s. The response to climate change is still hotly debated in Europe, but the debates are not about whether climate change is happening, but are rather centred on the size of CO_2-reduction targets and on the nature of political, societal and economic transformations that are needed to reduce energy use and carbon emissions. Climate change denial is receding in other countries around the world as well. Reviewing press reporting on climate scepticism in six countries over the period 2007–10, Manne (2012) found that while articles favouring or promoting denial actually grew throughout the period in the USA, they were virtually non-existent in the presses of China, France, Brazil and India. Climate denialists have been most active politically in the USA where climate denial is still regarded as a legitimate political position and is widely embraced by Americans, though there is evidence from recent polling that a combination of erratic and violent weather events in 2015 is contributing to reduced scepticism among the general public. Manne cites opinion polls which show that in 2008, 58 percent of Americans believed climate change is human related. This declined to 50 percent in 2010, but in a study in October 2015 published by the Guardian, 70 percent of those surveyed were confident in the science behind climate change, the highest level since 2008 (Guardian 2015c). This could mark a shift in the political legitimacy of climate denial.

Climate denial in the USA can be traced back to the first time that an accord on climate emission reductions was put on the international agenda at the United Nations Conference on Environment and Development in Rio de Janeiro in 1992. As noted in Chapter 4, then president of the USA, George Bush, and his negotiators played a key role in blocking an accord on CO_2 emissions. The USA then declined to sign the Kyoto Protocol in 2005 and in the intervening years has refused to go along with any concrete commitments to climate reductions. In the nascent presidential campaign in progress while this book was in its final stages, virtually all of the declared Republican presidential candidates are either sceptical to climate change or deny outright that there is a relationship between CO_2 emissions and climate. The US congress has long been dominated by climate sceptics and their scepticism can largely be attributed to a concern that American industrial competitiveness and profits will be affected by policies to reign in emissions.

There is ample evidence that this 'concern' is actively encouraged by industries and interest groups that benefit from fossil fuel capitalism and who regard the transformation that follows from an acknowledgement of climate change as an economic and ideological threat to their profits and political influence (Boykoff 2011). Conservative think tanks, foundations and research institutes such as the Global Climate Coalition, the Heritage Foundation, the American Enterprise Institute, the Competitive Enterprise Institute, the Cato Institute, the Heartland Institute and the Marshall Institute have published books denying that climate change is related to human activity. Several of these provide fellowships for denialist scientists (Barley 2010). According to Manne, the Marshall Institute and the Cato Institute consist of a hard core of 'Hayekian neoliberals who regarded arguments about the need for government regulation to health and environment as socialism and stealth' (2012: 3). Manne relates how these same institutes played a key supportive role in the tobacco industry's battle against government interventions to control and reduce tobacco sales. The industry and its researchers developed an effective research and discursive tactic used to stall political action on tobacco for decades: 'the manufacture of doubt' about the health consequences of cigarette smoking. This same discursive tactic has been used effectively in the campaign to keep government from engaging with climate change.

Representatives from the fossil fuel industries have been prominent funders of climate denial research. The coal billionaires Charles and David Koch have openly dedicated millions of dollars to climate denial research as well as to media campaigns and political candidates who raise questions about, or outright deny climate change. According to an accounting by Greenpeace, cited in the Guardian (2015a), the oil corporation Exxon concluded internally decades ago that carbon emissions were contributing to climate change, yet dedicated USD 30 million to research institutions over the ensuing years that promoted disinformation on climate change and donated millions of dollars to US congressmen to block climate change legislation. The efforts to generate opposition to climate legislation have been effective. In April 2011 a bill was introduced in the US House of Representatives to overturn the findings of the Environmental Protection Agency about the dangers of greenhouse emissions. The bill did not pass, but received unanimous Republican support (Goldenberg 2015). Much of the recent denial-related funding is linked to an interest in expanding oil and gas exploration, including the extraction of oil from shale oil and fracking, responsible for a recent renaissance in oil extraction in the USA, but, in addition to the release of carbon emissions, these processes have severe local environmental consequences, including the pollution of water sources from the chemicals used to extract the oil and the risk of earthquakes (Mitchell 2011). President Obama, who in 2015 began to speak more clearly and aggressively about the need to address climate change, still continues to support fracking and a continuation of oil exploration in Alaska and the Gulf of Mexico.

Another related source of climate denial is ideological. The proponents of neo-liberal capitalism see an admission of climate change as a threat to free-market, no-government governance. They rightly fear that an admission of the relationship between carbon emissions and climate change would open up a greater role of government in steering economic activity away from fossil fuels, stronger regulation of energy markets, and a realignment of subsidies to disfavour fossil fuels and favour renewable energies. Another effective discursive tactic has been to associate government intervention in society and economy of all kinds with the restriction of individual freedom. As Polanyi formulated it in his landmark book the Great Transformation (1957), 'Planning and control are being attacked as a denial of freedom. Free enterprise and private ownership are declared to be essentials of freedom. No society built on other foundations is said to deserve to be called free. The freedom that regulation creates is denounced as unfreedom: the justice, liberty and welfare it offers are decried as a camouflage of slavery' (cited in Harvey 2005: 37). This equation of freedom with free markets and an absent government continues to be brought to bear in political debates on climate action in the USA. However, as Polanyi implies, without collective rules and regulations, many essential freedoms and rights would be curtailed, including the right of future generations to a healthy ecosystem. The effects of climate change on ocean and land ecosystems will impinge on the freedom of large segments of the global population to continue their livelihoods, and for many others to have access to the food, medicinal products and other essential goods that they produce for their own subsistence. By denying climate change and denying the need for the governance of markets in order to reduce energy use and climate emissions, these and other essential freedoms will be curtailed. Barry (2007: 457) makes this point when he writes 'a shift away from "economic growth" and orthodox understandings of "prosperity" should be taken as an opportunity to redefine basic political and economic concepts. It asks us to consider the possibility that human freedom and a well-organised and governed polity does not depend, in any fundamental sense, on increasing levels of material affluence.'

Unfettered capitalism has also restricted economic freedoms to a large share of the population through the maldistribution of wealth. As Patel writes, 'Without cash in a market society, you're free to do nothing, to have very little and to die young...What needs to be plucked out of markets is the perpetual and overriding hunger for expansion and profit that has brought us to the brink of ecological catastrophe; what needs to be plucked out of us is the belief that markets are the only way to value our world (2009: 188). From a global perspective, in an increasingly interconnected global economy, the top 100 billionaires in the world added USD 240 billion to their wealth in one year (2012) alone (Harvey 2014: 166). Piketty's (2014) long term historical analysis of capitalism shows that the rich in capitalist societies are getting richer. According to research by Jones and Kammen (2011) in the USA, the carbon footprints of those with annual household incomes of over USD 120,000 are more than double those of households that earn less than USD 10,000. Research by Wilkenson and Pickett (2009) clearly shows that countries with the flattest distributions of wealth (least socio-economic differences between rich and poor) are those with the smallest environmental footprints. Putting the findings of Piketty and those of Wilson and Pickett together leads to the conclusion that the purest forms of capitalism are both socio-economically unjust and environmentally destructive. Prugh et al. (2000: 71) sum up the problem when they write that 'Capitalism... is fatally blind to...the maldistribution of the world's wealth, denies ethical obligations to community welfare, shifts all possible costs to others (including the public), seeks to co-opt the political process by means of moneyed interest groups and otherwise erodes and corrupts the public sphere'.

I agree with MacMullan (2013: 250) when he emphasizes the necessity of taking a pragmatic approach to the need for transformation: 'If pragmatism is the commitment that we can always improve ourselves and communities by using intelligence to find ever more flourishing and meaningful lives, the pragmatism will always be defined by its ability to refine, reclaim, and refuse the habits through which we actually live our lives'. The spectre of climate change demands that we lift ourselves above dogmatic ideological debates and acknowledge the pragmatic imperative that climate emissions cannot be reduced to the levels needed to avoid violent climate change in a capitalist, growth economy. As Mason (2015: 247) writes, 'The real absurdists are not the climate-change deniers, but the politicians and economists who believe that the existing market mechanisms can stop climate change, that the market must set the limits of climate action and that the market can be structured to deliver the biggest re-engineering project humanity has ever tried'.

It is precisely this pragmatic approach that is behind the many community efforts to reduce the environmental impacts discussed in Chapter 6. The challenge is to increase the scale and take this pragmatic step towards a low carbon society at the level of national governance. In Europe there is an increasing political acceptance across the spectrum from left to right that action is necessary and that it will require a role for government in steering markets towards renewable energies and greater efficiency. Nonetheless, as discussed in Chapter 6, there are still few signs that European countries are willing to dispense with economic growth as a political objective. In the USA, Klein argues that today's political class is 'wholly incapable' of implementing plans to respond to climate change and that doing so will involve 'unlearning the core tenets of the stifling free-market ideology that governed every state of their rise to power' (2014: 460). At least one member of the current political class, presidential candidate Bernie Sanders, has evidently unlearned these core tenets of free-market ideology. He is one of the few successful politicians in the history of the USA to declare himself a socialist and is the only declared socialist ever to be elected to the US Congress. In his nascent campaign for president he emphasizes the importance of correcting the USA's maldistribution of wealth, and in the first presidential debate when asked what he considered to be the greatest national security threat to the country, he named climate change. This security threat was echoed the following day by the French foreign minister Laurence Fabian, who designated the upcoming UN Convention on Climate as a conference for peace, drawing attention to climate-change consequences for migration and the risk of conflicts (Guardian 2015b).

Soft capitalism

As emphasized throughout the book, the politics and logic of capitalism are spreading to other parts of the world, including China and the former socialist economies of the Soviet Union and Eastern Europe. There are a few countries in Latin America that have held out against capitalist expansion. Cuba has a half-century history of anti-capitalist development, ranks highest of Latin American countries in the Human Development Index and has come further than most developing countries in achieving its Millennium Development Goals (Glennie 2011). More recently, Ecuador and Bolivia have attempted to foster alternative development models that emphasize the fostering of a healthy environment in national development. In Europe, the Nordic countries have fostered political economies in which the market logic of capitalism is held in check and where there are efforts to prioritize social and environmental welfare. The Nordic 'social democracies' have created political economies that can be characterized as 'soft capitalism' because of the strongly progressive tax system, the important place given labour unions in insuring worker rights and benefits such as pregnancy leave, long vacations, high taxes and strong redistributive tax policies, relatively high minimum wages and reasonable health care and education (Anderson 2007: 11). Interestingly, US presidential candidate Sanders is using the 'Nordic model' as a vision for transformation in the USA towards a less socio-economically divided society with a social safety net that includes universal health care and free higher education.

Sweden and Denmark have long been aggressive in prioritizing environmental protection and energy savings and have set ambitious targets for reductions of energy use and carbon emissions. Denmark managed to stabilize its energy growth after 1973, but this does not account for the fact that, along with other European countries, the products consumed in Denmark and the energy used to produce them are increasingly displaced to other parts of the world, principally China and other Asian countries, so that if these are accounted for the energy used to fuel growth in the Danish economy is actually increasing. Norway has an extensive hydropower-based electricity production which provides carbon-free energy, but a steady growth in electricity consumption, coupled with environmental regulations limiting the building of more dams and power stations means that Norway now regularly imports fossil fuel-generated electricity from the integrated European market. Relatively inexpensive 'clean' electricity is one of the reasons behind the growth of electric car ownership in Norway. Norwegians now have the highest per capita ownership of electric vehicles in the world. The government has offered incentives for electric cars such as value-added tax exemption, favourable parking conditions and the use of collective traffic lanes in commuting hours. This support for electric vehicles may make sense in an electricity production system based on renewables, but in the vast majority of countries in which electricity is produced by fossil fuels, the carbon-reduction benefits of this strategy are less evident. Also, the availability of this 'green' transport vehicle prolongs the car-centred transport vision for future mobility rather than one based on public transportation, walking and biking. There is now an intense debate in Oslo as to whether to extend the size of highways connecting Oslo with its suburbs due to significant traffic and congestion, part of which is due to the increased numbers of electric vehicles using and clogging up collective traffic lanes and making it difficult for buses to keep to their timetables. The public uproar over this has forced the government to reverse the policy of allowing electric vehicles to use collective lanes.

According to Ytterstad (2014), Norway is in its own form of denial because of its petroleum-based economy and attempts to justify continued oil exploration and production while at the same time arguing in global fora for the need for aggressive climate mitigation. The partly state-owned Statoil has made an effort to characterize Norwegian oil and gas exploration in sensitive Arctic environments as 'clean' relative to other countries, despite criticism from every major Norwegian environmental organization and the majority of the island communities where fishing and tourism would be most affected, Lofoton, Vesterålen and Senja (Skjærseth and Skodvin 2003; Ryggvik 2010 and 2013). In this soft capitalist country, the ecological footprint and carbon emissions per capita are both above the European average, having increased by 25 percent since 1990 (Midttun and Olsson 2011; World Bank 2005). Norwegian household habits are some of the most energy intensive in the world, attributable to high and growing per capita living space, high thermal comfort demands, high consumption of hot water and high per capita kilometres travelled, both by automobile and air. Norwegian consumption, measured by household expenditures adjusted for inflation, more than tripled between 1960 and 2010 (Strand and Thorsen 2013). Like capitalist countries everywhere, Norwegian and other Nordic economies are as intent on promoting economic growth as other OECD countries, but if growth in economy, consumption and energy-dependent habits are not curtailed, there will continue to be energy 'rebounds' that prevent deep reductions in energy use and climate emissions.

Breaking the habits of capitalism

The lesson from the Nordic experiences with partial state ownership of energy corporations, strong social welfare policies, strong doses of market and corporate regulation, a sense of collective responsibility for the provision of crucial services such as education, health and the environment demonstrate that this model can lead to within-capitalism amelioration of the carbon impacts of political economy. Still, with the integration of increasing numbers of the global population into the global growth economy, neither soft capitalism nor the greening of neo-liberal capitalism will be sufficient to bring carbon emissions down to the necessary levels. The vast majority of us living in the rich countries of the world are habituated to individual ownership and control, consuming on debt and decommissioning the active participation of our bodies in many of the central practices of everyday living. Breaking these habits will take an effort directed at every level of societal organization from national to community and household.

In concluding this book I want to make it clear that we need to change habits, not eliminate them. Habits will always be integrated to one extent or another in negotiating everyday tasks. The challenge we face from a low carbon perspective is that in the rich countries of the world, the actions involved in the performance of many everyday habits are using significant amounts of energy and emitting amounts of carbon far above what the ecosystem can tolerate. This has not been given sufficient attention in the academic analysis of low carbon transformation. We need to bring the epistemology of habit to the study of energy consumption. The subjects of analysis will include individual and collective histories of household and place, the agency in material structures of the house and in household technologies scripted for growth and high energy use, the know-how of household members, and how all of this is nested in collective norms, rules and social relations encouraging growth and discouraging sharing. A theory of habit suggests new policies for reducing carbon emissions. These would emphasize reducing and changing the nature of work; infra-structural and technological polices aimed at making collective transport more convenient and reasonable; reducing the size of homes; increasing the sharing of living spaces and products; and reducing the dependency of food consumption on refrigeration. Information about how to accomplish all of these would rely not just on information brochures and manuals, but on practical learning, demonstrations and experimentation. The intentional communities discussed in Chapter 6 are an important source of information on habit transformation and the ways it can be approached in low carbon policy. Important experiments are taking place with collective solutions for work, food, housing and transport as well as with local currencies and informal economies. The energy and environ-mental consequences of these efforts need to be examined, as well as their potential for scaling up.

As the final paragraphs are being written for this book, there are signs that a few key world leaders are finally taking climate action seriously. China and Brazil have announced for the first time that they intend to set aggressive carbon-reduction goals. The presidents of several European countries and of the USA have made aggressive statements on the need for action on climate change in the build up to the next round of climate talks in Paris at COP21 in November 2015. This is not the first time that courageous and ambitious statements are made in advance of a climate conference, only to be diluted into toothless action plans. Time will tell whether this 21st convening of an inter-national conference on climate will mark a change and result in ambitious emission-reduction targets. Concerning transforming the political economy of capitalism, the efforts in Europe to define and operationalize a circular economy, even if they retain economic growth as a political economic goal in their current form, are an interesting challenge to capitalist extractivism, pro-duct turnover and consumerism. At the community level, the eco-community and internet-based efforts to share services and products are enabling new habits and may represent an erosion of capitalism from the bottom. These experiments in political economy and everyday living may well be the first steps along a path to a new political economy that puts the ecology, human wellbeing and social welfare first; still if we as a global community are to take those extra steps needed to dramatically reduce the carbon associated with human activity we will need to engage with, break and reform the habits of capitalist expansion.

References

Altvater, Elmer. 2007. The Social and Natural Environment of Fossil Capitalism. *Social Register* 43: 37–59.

Anderson, M. S. 2007. An Introductory Note on the Environmental Economics of the Circular Economy. *Sustainability Science* 2(1):133–140.

Barley, S. R. 2010. Building an Institutional Field to Corral a Government: A Case to Set an Agenda for Organizational Studies. *Organizational Studies* 31(6): 777–805.

Barry, John. 2007. Towards a Model of Green Political Economy: From Ecological Modernisation to Economic Security. *International Journal of Green Economics* 1(3/4): 446–464.

Boykoff, Maxwell T. 2011. *Who Speaks for the Climate? Making Sense of Media Reporting on Climate Change*. Cambridge: Cambridge University Press.

Glennie, Jonathan. 2011. Cuba: A Development Model that Proved the Doubters Wrong. Guardian. Available at http://www.theguardian.com/global-development/poverty-ma tters/2011/aug/05/cuban-development-model. Accessed 20 August 2015.

Goldenberg, Suzanne. 2015a. ExxonMobil Gave Millions to Climate-Denying Law-makers despite Pledge. Available at http://readersupportednews.org/news-section2/ 312-16/31300-exxonmobil-gave-millions-to-climate-denying-lawmakers-despite-pledge. Accessed 24 July 2015.

Guardian. 2015a. ExxonMobil Gave Millions to Climate-Denying Lawmakers despite Pledge. Available at http://www.theguardian.com/environment/2015/jul/15/exxon-m obil-gave-millions-climate-denying-lawmakers. Accessed 10 August 2015.

Guardian. 2015b. France Warns of Security Risks caused by Global Warming. Available at http://www.theguardian.com/environment/2015/oct/14/france-warns-of-security-risks-caused-by-global-warming. Accessed 18 October 2015.

Guardian. 2015c. Rising Numbers of Americans Believe Climate Science, Poll Shows. Available at http://www.theguardian.com/environment/2015/oct/13/rising-numbers-of-american-believe-climate-science-poll-shows. Accessed 18 October 2015.

Hamilton, Clive. 2003. *Growth Fetish*. London: Pluto Press.

Harvey, David. 2005. *A Brief History of Neoliberalism*. Oxford: Oxford University Press.

Harvey, David. 2014. *Seventeen Contradictions and the End of Capitalism*. Oxford and New York: Oxford University Press.

Jones, Christopher and Daniel Kammen. 2011. Quantifying Carbon Footprint Reduction Opportunities for U.S. Households and Communities. *Environmental Science and Technology* 45(9): 4088–4095.

Klein, Naomi. 2014. *This Changes Everything: Capitalism vs. the Climate*. New York: Simon and Shuster.

MacMullan, Terrance. 2013. The Fly Wheel of Society: Habit and Social Meliorism in the Pragmatist Tradition. In Tom Sparrow and Adam Hutchinson (eds), *A History of Habit: From Aristotle to Bourdieu*. Lanham, MD: Lexington Books, pp. 229–255.

Manne, Robert. 2012. A Dark Victory: How Vested Interests Defeated Climate Science. *Monthly* (Australia), August: 23–29.

Mason, Paul. 2015. *PostCapitalism: A Guide to Our Future*. London: Allen Lane.

Midttun, Atle and Lennart Olsson. 2011. The Nordic Model and Ecology: High Rhetoric and Mediocre Practice. In Atle Midttun and Nina Witoszek (eds), *The Nordic Model: Is It Sustainable and Exportable?* Oslo: Norwegian School of Business Management and University of Oslo. Available at www.tendencias21.net/attachment/257857. Accessed 17 August 2015.

Mitchell, Timothy. 2011. *Carbon Democracy: Political Power in the Age of Oil*. London and New York: Verso.

Patel, Raj. 2009. *The Value of Nothing: How to Reshape Market Society and Redefine Democracy*. New York: Picador.

Piketty, Thomas. 2014. *Capital in the Twenty-First Century*. Cambridge, MA: Belknap Press of Harvard University Press.

Polanyi, Karl. 1957. *The Great Transformation*. Boston, MA: Beacon Press.

Prugh, Thomas, Robert Cosntanza and Herman Daly. 2000. *The Local Politics of Global Sustianability*. Washington, DC: Island Press.

Ryggvik, Helge. 2010. *Til Siste Dråpe om Oljens Politiske Økonomi*. Oslo: Aschehoug.

Ryggvik, Helge. 2013. *Norsk Olje og Klima*. Oslo: Gylendal Akademisk.

Skjærseth, Jon and Tora Skodvin. 2003. *Climate Change and the Oil Industry: Common Problems, Varying Strategies*. Manchester: Manchester University Press.

Strand, Pål and Lotte Rustad Thorsen. 2013. Forbruksundersøkelsen 2102. Report published by the Norwegian Central Bureau of Statistics. Available at https://www.ssb.no/fbu/. Accessed 19 October 2015.

Van Greithuysen, Pascal. 2010. Why Are We Growth Addicted? The Hard Way towards Degrowth in the Involutionary Western Development Path. *Journal of Cleaner Production* 18: 590–595.

Weltzner, Harald. 2011. *Mental Infrastructures: How Growth Entered the World and Our Souls*. Berlin: Heinrich-Boll-Stiftung.

Wilkenson, R. G. and K. Pickett. 2009. *The Spirit Level: Why More Equal Societies almost Always Do Better*. London: Allen Lane.

World Bank. 2005. CO2 Emissions (Metric Tons per Capita). Available at http://data.worldbank.org/indicator/EN.ATM.CO2E.PC. Accessed 29 September 2015.

Ytterstad, Andreas. 2014. Good Sense on Global Warming. *International Socialism: A Quarterly Review of Social Theory* 144. Available at http://isj.org.uk/good-sense-on-global-warming/. Accessed 15 October 2015.

Index

Aarts, H. 25–6
accumulation 7, 9–10
actions: future actions and experiential knowledge 24, 25, 26, 28; and institutions 26; material and human agency 29; role of the body 27; as shaped by material objects 29–30; technologies and delegation of work/know-how 30–1; technologies of action 23–4
advertising: personal cleanliness products 48–9; and planned obsolescence 78; power of 16
Africa 115
agency: household appliances and lack of bodily agency 30–1; material actions and human agency 29; theory of 24
Agyeman, J. 103
air conditioning: carbon emissions 45–6; in cars 47; commercial buildings 48; energy consumption 48; EU support for energy-efficient units 68; increased use, India 46–7; increased use, Vietnam 47; and personal comfort 48; see also heating/cooling, domestic
Altvater, E. 5, 7, 8, 119
American Society of Heating, Refrigerating and Air-Conditioning Engineers (ASHRAE) 32–3
Amin, S. 6, 10
Arndt, H. W. 10
Ashenburg, K. 48–9, 50
Attali, S. 112
Australia 48, 50

Banerjee, S. 13
Barry, J. 64, 70, 122
bathrooms 49–50
behavioural economics 23

behaviouralist theories 22–3
Bianchi, C. 75
Birtwistle. G. 75
Blundorn, I 2
bodies: bathroom numbers and sizes 49–50; bodily transformation and comfort control 47; body-near practices 27; cleanliness, changing practices of 48–9; cleanliness and product availability 49, 51–2; clothes washing 30–1, 50–1; frequency of bathing 50; and habit formation 27–8; household appliances and lack of bodily agency 30–1; mind/body separation 25, 28–9, 35; see also comfort; embodiment
body techniques 27
Botsman, R. 111
bottom-up movements: importance of 103; need for institutional support for 88
Bourdieu, Pierre: collective element of habit 35; embodiment of knowledge 25; experiential knowledge 27–8; habitus and dispositions 24, 27; practical knowledge 27; symbolic violence concept 86–7
Brazil 13, 72, 126
BRICS (Brazil, Russia, India, China and South Africa) 13
building comfort bubbles 31–2, 33; see also comfort
Burawoy, Michael 11, 87
Busch, J. F. 33

capital: accumulation of 7, 9–10; nature as 6–7, 119
capitalism: challenges to 87–8; as common sense 15–16; culture of (consumption) 16; defined 6; within ecological critiques 78–9; evolution of 9–10;

110–11; importance of 103, 126; local initiatives, Local Agenda 21 95–6; Low Impact Development (LID) movment 110; non-growth orientation of 103, 106; scaling-up potential 114–15; transition movement 107–9
Intergovernmental Panel on Climate Change (IPCC) 1
international development organizations 12
Ireland 65

Jack, T. 50
Jackson, T. 77–8
James, William 25, 35
Japan: domestic heating/cooling practices 34, 46; new clothing practices 48; urban gardens 113
Jevons, William S. 69–70
Jones, C. 43, 122

Kallis, G. 77, 103
Kammen, D. 43, 122
Kapper, J. L. 56
Kasper, D. 109–10
Kennedy, Robert 93–4
Keynesian principles 11
Klein, N. 5, 11, 114, 119, 123
knowledge: embodied 25, 27–8, 35; experiential and dispositions for future actions 25, 26, 28; forms of, social practice theory 23–4; inarticulate knowledge 25; practical knowledge 27; tacit knowledge 24, 25
Koch, Charles 121
Koch, David 121
Krueger, R. 103

labour: monetary payments for 90, 92; productivity demands (prosperity vs. growth) 77–8, 90–1; waged/non-waged distinction 9; worker benefits 91; working hours 91–2
Lafferty, W. 96
Larsen, M. 56
Latin America: alternative community movements 110; capitalist expansion in 123; commercial forestry activities 73–4; neo-liberal capitalism in 11
Layard, R. 77
LeBlanc, D. 63
Lietaert, M. 105–6
Lifkin, K. 108, 109
Local Agenda 21 initiatives 95–6, 108

local transformative movements 88
low carbon transformation: and changing habits 125–6; community and collaborative practices 114–15; as crisis for democracy 98–9; denial and resistance to 119–20; labour relations 90–2; provision-production-consumption synergies 88–90; role of materiality 29; strong environmental governance 92–5, 99
Low Impact Development (LID) movement 110
Lutzenhiser, L. 32

MacMullan, T. 122
Manne, R. 120–1
market environmentalism 64
marketization 6
Martinez-Alier, J. 77
Marx, Karl 7, 10, 86
Mason, P. 65, 123
Massey, D. 16
materiality: automobility habits 53; displacement of know-how 30–1; of domestic heating/cooling 32–4; material scripting of action 29
Mauss, Marcel 25, 27, 28
Maxey, M. 103, 110
meat consumption 56
middle classes 15–16, 40
Mignolo, W. D. 115
Mitchell, T. 119
Murphey, M. 33, 47
Mylan, J. 50–1

Nader, L. 22
Nailing, Y, 74
Narain, S. 73
nature, capitalization of 6–7, 119
Navarez, R. 9, 35
neo-liberal capitalism: Chile experiment 11–12; climate change denial and 121–2; and economic liberalization of India 14; evolution of 11; global extension of 11–12; normalization of, USA 15
New Economics Foundation (NEC) 91
New Zealand 67
Nielsen, K. 47, 52
Nordic social democracies 124
Norway: average house sizes 42; building cooperatives 105; consumption rebound effect 70; deregulation of energy systems 67; electric cars 124; electricity

Taylor & Francis eBooks

Helping you to choose the right eBooks for your Library

Add Routledge titles to your library's digital collection today. Taylor and Francis ebooks contains over 50,000 titles in the Humanities, Social Sciences, Behavioural Sciences, Built Environment and Law.

Choose from a range of subject packages or create your own!

Benefits for you
- » Free MARC records
- » COUNTER-compliant usage statistics
- » Flexible purchase and pricing options
- » All titles DRM-free.

Benefits for your user
- » Off-site, anytime access via Athens or referring URL
- » Print or copy pages or chapters
- » Full content search
- » Bookmark, highlight and annotate text
- » Access to thousands of pages of quality research at the click of a button.

eCollections – Choose from over 30 subject eCollections, including:

Archaeology	Language Learning
Architecture	Law
Asian Studies	Literature
Business & Management	Media & Communication
Classical Studies	Middle East Studies
Construction	Music
Creative & Media Arts	Philosophy
Criminology & Criminal Justice	Planning
Economics	Politics
Education	Psychology & Mental Health
Energy	Religion
Engineering	Security
English Language & Linguistics	Social Work
Environment & Sustainability	Sociology
Geography	Sport
Health Studies	Theatre & Performance
History	Tourism, Hospitality & Events

For more information, pricing enquiries or to order a free trial, please contact your local sales team:
www.tandfebooks.com/page/sales